Start-up Actions and Outcomes: What Entrepreneurs Do to Reach Profitability

Start-up Actions and Outcomes: What Entrepreneurs Do to Reach Profitability

Paul D. Reynolds
Aston Business School
United Kingdom
pauldavidsonreynolds@gmail.com

the essence of knowledge

Boston — Delft

Foundations and Trends® in Entrepreneurship

Published, sold and distributed by:
now Publishers Inc.
PO Box 1024
Hanover, MA 02339
United States
Tel. +1-781-985-4510
www.nowpublishers.com
sales@nowpublishers.com

Outside North America:
now Publishers Inc.
PO Box 179
2600 AD Delft
The Netherlands
Tel. +31-6-51115274

The preferred citation for this publication is

P. D. Reynolds. *Start-up Actions and Outcomes: What Entrepreneurs Do to Reach Profitability.* Foundations and Trends® in Entrepreneurship, vol. 12, no. 6, pp. 443–559, 2016.

This *Foundations and Trends®* issue was typeset in LaTeX using a class file designed by Neal Parikh. Printed on acid-free paper.

ISBN: 978-1-68083-228-0
© 2016 P. D. Reynolds

Foundations and Trends® in Entrepreneurship
Volume 12, Issue 6, 2016
Editorial Board

Editorial Scope

Topics

Foundations and Trends® in Entrepreneurship publishes survey and tutorial articles in the following topics:

- Nascent and start-up entrepreneurs
- Opportunity recognition
- New venture creation process
- Business formation
- Firm ownership
- Market value and firm growth
- Franchising
- Managerial characteristics and behavior of entrepreneurs
- Strategic alliances and networks

- Government programs and public policy
- Gender and ethnicity
- New business financing
- Family-owned firms
- Management structure, governance and performance
- Corporate entrepreneurship
- High technology
- Small business and economic growth

Information for Librarians

Foundations and Trends® in Entrepreneurship, 2016, Volume 12, 6 issues. ISSN paper version 1551-3114. ISSN online version 1551-3122. Also available as a combined paper and online subscription.

Foundations and Trends® in Entrepreneurship
Vol. 12, No. 6 (2016) 443–559
© 2016 P. D. Reynolds
DOI: 10.1561/0300000071

Start-up Actions and Outcomes: What Entrepreneurs Do to Reach Profitability

Paul D. Reynolds*
Aston Business School
United Kingdom
pauldavidsonreynolds@gmail.com

*Comments of the editors and an anonymous reviewer were the basis for substantial improvements in the presentation and were much appreciated. The author, however, is fully responsible for all errors of commission or omission.

Contents

Abstract

Globally, hundreds of millions enter the firm creation process every year. About a third will actually develop a profitable new firm. Understanding how these successful efforts reach initial profits has been a major challenge for entrepreneurial scholars. A recently developed research protocol has involved systematic collection of data on the start-up activities of representative samples of nascent ventures and tracking their outcomes; a number of Panel Study of Entrepreneurial Dynamics [PSED] projects have been completed. Assembling data from five PSED cohorts in four countries has allowed for attention to the effect of start-up activities on the outcomes of a harmonized sample of 2,500 nascent ventures. There is no difference in outcomes related to the gender of the nascent entrepreneur, a small effect associated with age, and modest impacts associated with educational attainment, work history, and experience with other start-up initiatives. There is a systematic country effect; the U.S. has a lower proportion of profitable new firms than Australia, China, or Sweden. Many aspects of the start-up effort are related to the outcomes. A greater range of start-up activities early in the start-up process is associated with profitability, less terminations, and fewer with a long tenure in the start-up process. Activities emphasizing promotion of the nascent venture, assembling a firm infrastructure, and implementing a production process are associated with initial profitability and fewer terminations. Business planning increases the tendency to quit and reduces the proportion active in the start-up process. It may reduce the time to reach disengagement. Implementing of promotion, infrastructure development, and establishing a production process also reduces the time to reach initial profits. The results have implications for both aspiring entrepreneurs and policy development.

P. D. Reynolds. *Start-up Actions and Outcomes: What Entrepreneurs Do to Reach Profitability*. Foundations and Trends® in Entrepreneurship, vol. 12, no. 6, pp. 443–559, 2016.

DOI: 10.1561/0300000071

1

Introduction

Business creation, a fundamental feature of entrepreneurship, is not only widespread, with over 250 million efforts in place around the world, it is a core aspect of modern market economies.[1] New firms are a major source of new jobs, economic innovation and adaptation, as well as a major career option for hundreds of millions.[2] There is now substantial interest in facilitating firm creation by political leaders at all levels of government in all parts of the world, to say nothing of the strong attraction for millions of young adults exploring work career options. This has led to considerable efforts to promote business creation by educational institutions, government agencies, not for profits, and international organization. A substantial commercial sector facilitating entrepreneurship has also emerged.

Business creation can be considered a two-stage process. The first stage, entry into the start-up process, begins when individuals or a team takes action to create a new business. The second stage involves the efforts to create a profitable firm, which is completed by a transition to

---

[1] Estimates of the scope of participation are provided in Reynolds (2012, 2015a).

[2] Summary overview by Van Praag and Versloot, 2007. A recent assessment on job creation is provided by Lawless (2014).

3

profitability or disengagement. While a number of factors may affect achieving profitability, most would assume that what is done in the start-up process has a major effect. There is no shortage of books, programs, seminars, workshops, media experts, and the like standing ready to offer advice on how entrepreneurs should proceed. This mass of cheerleaders and coaches find it exciting and profitable to promote entrepreneurship, particularly if someone else bears the risks.

But what is the risk? What proportion of those coordinating people, resources, and ideas to implement a new venture actually reach profitability? The best available evidence suggests that only one in three active in business creation achieve initial profits after six years.[3]

The majority of start-up efforts, therefore, do not reach profitability. While the positive impact of vigorous business creation on economic growth is widely recognized, the total social cost of the entrepreneurial sector is not well understood. And until a nascent venture reach profitability, the owners—and sponsors—will not recoup their financial investments and the start-up team will have little—except experience—to show for their sweat equity. An analysis of the early years of the sunk costs associated with two U.S. cohorts of nascent ventures found that 80% of the time and money invested in start-ups were in ventures that did not achieve profitability a year after entering the process.[4] While the average invested in still-born start-ups is less than those achieving profitability, the much larger number of initiatives leads to a larger aggregate sunk costs.

But the development of effective educational procedures and public policies to promote firm creation has been hampered by little reliable knowledge about the entrepreneurial process. There is little solid information on a wide range of issues, such as:

- What proportion of start-up efforts reach initial profits?

---

[3]This is consistent with a recent global assessment comparing the prevalence of those in the pre-profit phase with the prevalence of those managing a new firm, profitable for up to 18 months (Bergmann and Stephan, 2012). Across 48 countries there were about three nascent entrepreneurs in the pre-profit stage for each new firm owner.

[4]Reynolds and Curtin (2009).

- How long does it take to determine the outcome after entering business creation?

- What do start-up teams do to implement new firms?[5]

- What is unique about efforts that become profitable new firms?

The major complication has been the absence of reliable, detailed descriptions of representative samples of nascent ventures during the start-up process. This would involve longitudinal data collection that tracks a cohort of nascent ventures from the beginning, when the first steps are taken to implement a new firm, to the final resolution, when the initiative has either reached initial profits or been abandoned by the start-up team. Such projects have now been completed and this unique resource is the basis for the following analysis.

The primary objective of this assessment is to provide a description of the firm creation process based on five harmonized data sets from four countries that track the business creation process. As all are based on representative samples, this is an unprecedented portrayal.

The second objective is to explore the role of start-up activities on the outcomes for these nascent ventures. Outcomes include not only whether they reach profitability or disengage but how long it takes to achieve a resolution. The sooner a start-up team can determine if a nascent venture is profitable or hopeless the lower the sunk costs.

The presentation begins with a review of the conceptualization of business creation, followed by a discussion of assessments of the role of business planning, the start-up activity that has received the most attention in relation to outcomes. A summary of the Panel Study of Entrepreneurial Dynamics (PSED) protocol describes the basis for the five cohort data set. Description of the outcomes reported in the first 72 months after entering the start-up process clarifies the nature of the dependent variables. Presenting the prevalence and timing of 19 activities associated with the start-up process provides a unique, detailed

---

[5]There is an enormous literature of participant observation of "firms in development," often gathering much retrospective information, using samples of convenience (Mueller, Volery, and von Siemens, 2012). The following assessment is distinctive in utilizing representative samples of nascent ventures.

description of how nascent teams pursue business creation. Attention to the effect of specific activities on the outcomes indicates the presence of complex interrelationships. A factor analysis is the basis for multi-item indices that represent six domains of start-up activity. All start-up domains have a significant relationship to the outcomes and the time required to reach an outcome.

To identify the impact of different background factors and start-up domains on outcomes two assessments are completed. First, linear additive models are developed using stepwise regression. Second, interactions among factors are identified using a three level decision tree assessment. In both there are major differences related to the host country and the total amount of start-up activity. To identify the impact of specific start-up domains, the assessments are replicated without measures of total start-up activity. The final section summarizes the major patterns and the implications for those starting new firms, developing public policy, or planning the next stages of research.

Most analysis of start-up activity that may affect outcomes has focused on the development of business plans. Most of this, however, has considered business planning in isolation; there has been little research comparing the implementation of business planning in relation to the impact of other activities associated with the start-up process. The following assessment indicates a statistically significant relationship between business planning and outcomes, but with less impact than other start-up activities. Efforts to determine customer acceptance and organize a new venture appears to be have more impact on the outcomes. The major benefit of business planning appears to be on reducing the time required to reach an outcome. It is highly associated with speeding up decisions to abandon a start-up venture.

2

Conceptualizing Firm Creation

There is a lot of attention given to factors that may encourage business creation, such as market characteristics, macro-economic conditions, regional attributes, national research and development intensity, business opportunities, financing availability, positive entrepreneurial climate, supportive social networks, and speeches by politicians. But ultimately firms are created when individuals decide to take personal action to create a business. This conceptualization is presented in Figure 2.1.

There are several critical features of this model. First, it focuses on individuals that may be identified from the adult population. These are individual nascent entrepreneurs starting a business on their own and those working for existing firms, nascent intrapreneurs starting a business as part of their job. Once identified, they are able to report on the start-up venture, which may reflect their own individual efforts or that of a team. The data may be considered to represent a single nascent entrepreneur or a single nascent venture.

A considerable amount of research has emerged focusing on the effect of business planning on outcomes, broadly defined. Many of these assessments, particularly related to business planning, are not precise about a number of conceptual or operational definitions. Most

7

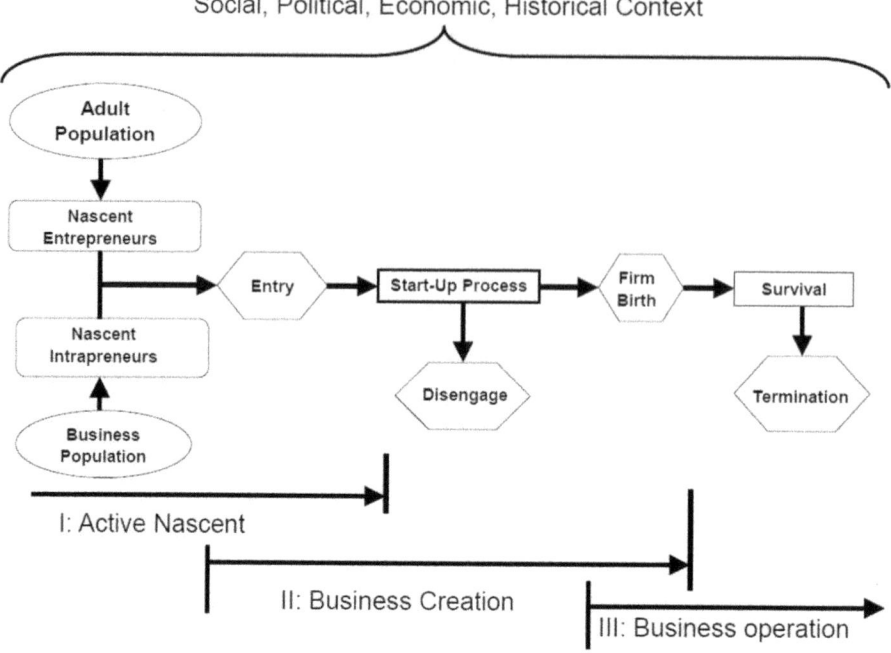

Figure 2.1: The Business Creation Process.

important is clarifying stages of the firm life course, as abstract concepts:

- Pre-entry: An individual or team may be considering business creation, but no activity to develop a new firm has taken place.

- Business creation phase: An individual or team is actively involved in the business creation process, initiating a range of activities considered relevant to the development of a profitable business.

- Business operation: A set of activities that assembles resources or components and delivers same to one or more customers in such a way that the total costs is less than the income received.

- Disengaged: No individuals or activities are associated with the production of goods or services.

For precise analysis clear operational definitions are required that will make a distinction between these different stages. A number of versions of such definitions have been developed for the different transitions.

For this assessment, a business venture is considered as a focus of economic activity or the coordination of resources, people and activities to provide economic value. This suggests that the primary role of the entrepreneur, or the entrepreneurial team, is to manage the balance of inducements and contributions to provide a net gain for the venture. While the emerging business may develop a bureaucratic form with explicit objectives, formalized resource management, well defined boundaries, and precise exchange relationships, this degree of structure is not typically present as a start-up begins to develop initial profits.[1]

---

[1]The conception of effective organizations as a locus of activity is developed in *The Functions of the Executive* (Barnard, 1951). The bureaucratic form, developed by Weber (1978), has been applied to emerging businesses by Katz and Gartner (1988) and considered with regards to the PSED data by Bush, Manolova, and Edelman (2008).

3

Entry into Business Creation

Substantial work has been completed on who is likely to be involved in business and many patterns are universal.[1] While there is no social category of individuals that are never involved in business creation, some people are much more likely to be involved. For example, men are generally more active than women, except for the least developed countries where there is gender parity. The increased activity among those 25 to 44 years old is a global pattern, those 18 to 24 and 45 to 54 years old are somewhat less active and participation drops dramatically for those over 55 years old. In developed countries, those that have not completed secondary or high school are generally less involved in business creation; in developing countries, however, those less educated are more involved that their more educated age-peers.[2] Perhaps most significant, from 70% to 80% of active nascent entrepreneurs pursue

---

[1]See Delmar and Davidsson (2000) for a review of patterns for Sweden, Reynolds et al. (2004) for a description for the United States, and any of the annual global reports or national reports developed as part of the Global Entrepreneurship Monitor program (www.gemconsortium.org) for international patterns. A novel effort to explore the nature of U. S. nascent entrepreneurs summarizes questionnaire data on 590 cases as "conversations" (Campbell and Nardi, 2009).

[2]Reynolds (2012).

a new firm while they have a job or are managing another firm. In many cases the new venture may compete with the existing venture, but others will focus on a different economic sector or market.

But businesses are created. Those that want a business realize they must take action to put a new firm in place. There are two unknowns regarding the start-up efforts. First, what do people actually do in creating a business? Second, what action strategies are the most effective for those in the start-up process? There have been a number of efforts to approach these issues, often focusing on intentions[3] or cognitive factors.[4] Assessments of the volume, clustering, and timing of start-up activities leading to more new ventures have been interpreted in relation to complexity theory;[5] this does not provide much attention to specific activities and, hence, guidance for nascent entrepreneurs. Efforts to distinguish between the focus of technologically based and other ventures has identified some differences.[6]

3.1   Starting a Business: Role of Business Planning

While there are many activities that can facilitate business creation, development of a business plan has received the majority of scholarly attention. This reflects, in part, the inclusion of strategies for other start-up activities as part of a business plan. This is the core content of the entire range of publications, from those prepared for the mass market to the graduate level MBA courses. The central feature of all is the formalized "business plan." A document that should be prepared to identify the objectives for the effort, the resources required to achieve same, a work plan for implementation, and a best guess of the balance among the different components. All of these components, of course, will differ for a new business in different economic sectors, with different competitive environments, in different social and political contexts, and with different access to resources.

---

[3]Hopp and Sonderegger (2015).
[4]Gatewood, Shaver, and Gartner (1995).
[5]Liao, Welsch, and Tan (2005), Lichtenstein et al. (2007).
[6]Liao and Welsch (2008)

When aspiring entrepreneurs participate in workshops, seminars, college courses, or degree programs designed to facilitate their efforts at business creation, the end product is almost always a written business plan. These are considered to (1) facilitate decision making by clarifying what information may be missing, (2) facilitate managing the resources required to implement a business, and (3) define clear objectives and a work plan for putting the new firm in place.[7] A formalized written business plan will facilitated interaction with others that may contribute to firm creation, such as financial institutions, government agencies, potential employees, suppliers and the like.[8] But this focus implies that without some type of written blueprint, a firm will not be created.[9]

The alternative perspective suggests that the time spent on creating a formalized business plan may not be well spent, as the necessary information may not be available without some action (such as testing the customer acceptance for the products) and premature formalization can lead to a narrow orientation that may overlook promising opportunities.[10] This perspective suggests that business planning is one of a range of activities may promote firm creation and success and may not be a necessary precondition, at least not for all new ventures. It has been suggested that such multi-faceted approach is particularly appropriate for nascent ventures emphasizing technological innovations, where the market for the output may not be well defined.[11] It is the basis for an extensive program, the I-Corp initiative, designed to train teams to implement new high technology firms, sponsored by the National Science Foundation.[12]

---

[7]Delmar and Shane (2003).

[8]Honig and Karlsson (2004).

[9]A recent exchange over the capacity to replicate findings with a Swedish data set reflects a shared commitment to testing hypotheses with empirical data, but the narrow focus on only business planning as a relevant start-up activity suggests that a broader perspective might be of value (Delmar and Shane, 2003, 2004; Honig and Karlsson, 2004; Honig and Samuelsson, 2014, 2015; Delmar, 2015a,b; Davidsson, 2015).

[10]Brinckmann et al. (2010).

[11]Osterwalder and Pigneur (2013); Reiss (2011).

[12]National Science Foundation (2016).

The importance and impact of business planning has been the subject of a number of reviews. One summarized 51 studies with comparable measures of outcomes on small firms, of which that 15 with less than 8 years of operational experience were considered "new firms." The primary focus was on measures of outcome associated with existing business.[13] Little attention was given to the role of planning in the transition from start-up to initial profitability.[14] More relevant is an effort to summarize eleven studies using longitudinal data covering the start-up to operational transition, using three measures of business planning and six different outcome measures.[15] A review of 50 relationships with a time lag suggest benefits from planning in 38% of the assessments, no impact in 60%, and a negative impact in 2% (1 case).

This body of research reflects a lack of precision on many issues. Most important is the concept of a business plan—or business planning.[16] But virtually all those that pursue business creation develop a plan as part of the start-up process, even if it is only in the form of a mental image of how to proceed. A formalized, written document, however, may not be the first thing that receives attention. Information gathering about a number of issues, such as customer appeal and input costs, may take precedence. Further, a plan that is developed and then slavishly followed until an outcome is determined is rare. In most cases they are likely to be a flexible guideline that is adjusted as other activities are pursued and new information is developed about resources, customers and potential opportunities.

---

[13] A good example is the analysis of 422 ventures identified as "new" on the basis of recent inclusions into telephone directories (Burke, Fraser, and Greene, 2010). No efforts to establish a precise date for "starting" or "establishing" the business is reported; it would appear that respondents provided their own operational definitions of these critical transitions.

[14] Brinckmann, Grichnik, and Kapsa (2010).

[15] Davidsson and Gordon (2012).

[16] A theoretical assessment of the value of business planning treated it as a dichotomous event, present or absent, and speculated on the impact for "success," also treated as dichotomous (Chwolka and Raith, 2012). The lack of empirical support for this modeling exercise is not unexpected.

3.2 A Broader Assessment

There is also variation in the outcomes that may be affected by business planning. For established, operational firms this has included the magnitude of sales, measures of profitability, as well as actual survival, indicated by avowing bankruptcy.[17] The effect on continuing with the start-up effort, initial sales, or reaching profitability have been utilized in assessing impacts on business creation.[18]

While continued operations and improved profitability are important aspects of the firm life course, there has been less attention to other benefits, such as reducing the time to reach an outcome. Given that the majority of firm creation efforts do not reach initial profits, this can be an important benefit. The sooner a decision about the future of the venture can be made, the lower the cost in time and money that will be devoted to the start-up process. A reduction in the sunk costs associated with the firm creation process and which cannot be recovered is a major benefit.

There are a wide range of activities that may be required to start a business in addition to an explicit business plan.[19] It is possible to pursue firm creation with an informal strategy, reflected in the implementation of start-up activities that have been initiated. Prior to the PSED protocol, discussed below, there were a few attempts to identify a range of activities beyond business planning.[20] However, most of the analysis has emphasized business planning to the exclusion of other activities that might facilitate business creation.

The unique feature of the following assessment is the implementation of precise measure of the critical transitions, tracking the impact of a wide range of start-up activities, and the utilization of five harmonized data sets that represent business creation in four countries.

---

[17]Brinckmann et al. (2010)

[18]Davidsson and Gordon (2012).

[19]One assessment of the success for 96 Ugandan entrepreneurs considered five start-up activities in addition to business planning (Gielnik et al., 2014).

[20]Gatewood, Shaver, and Gartner (1995) is a rare exception.

4

Tracking Business Creation: The PSED Protocol

Projects to identify nascent entrepreneurs in the early stages of business creation have been developed and implemented in a number of countries. They have used the Panel Study of Entrepreneurial Dynamics [PSED] protocol, named after the titles of the two U.S. projects.[1] Over a dozen projects have been implemented since 1995.[2] Five projects in four countries (Australia, China, Sweden, and two in the United States) have harmonized many aspects of the research design and the results assembled in a single, consolidated data set.[3] Each cohort is based on a sample representative of the business creation activity in the host country. As the cohorts represent business creation in a diverse set of national contexts, it is possible to have confidence that the same results

---

[1]PSED protocol data has been widely utilized in the study of entrepreneurship and business creation (Frid, 2015). One effort to use citation analysis identifies its central role in writings on entrepreneurship (Ramos-Rodriguez et al., 2015); a second citation assessment focusing on authors rather than data sources does not (Meyer et al., 2014).

[2]Projects in Australia, Canada, China, Germany, Latvia, Netherlands, Norway, Sweden and the United States are summarized in Reynolds and Curtin (2009).

[3]Described in Reynolds et al. (2016). This effort addresses some of the issues associated with maximizing the benefits of the PSED research programs is discussed in Gartner and Shaver (2012).

would be found in other countries. This data set can be utilized to examine the major features of the firm creation process. A summary is provided in Appendix A.

Locating a representative sample of those active in business creation begins with a representative sample of non-institutionalized adults. Those in prisons, hospitals, mental institutions, or living in student dormitories[4] are normally not screened. All others—regardless of their status in the labor force—are asked questions to determine if they consider themselves involved in business creation. After 2005 most projects utilized three items:

- Are you, alone or with others, involved in starting a business?

- Are you, alone or with others, involved in starting a business for your employer as part your normal job responsibilities?

- Are you an owner-manager of a business?

Those that answered yes to any or all of these items are then asked further questions to determine if they had engaged in some start-up activity in the past year, expected to own all or part of the business, and the venture had not reached profitability. Those actively involved as potential owners with an initiative that had not reached profitability were considered nascent entrepreneurs involved with a nascent venture. Depending on the project, they may receive from three to six follow-up interviews, providing a description of a multi-year segment of the firm life course.[5]

The major advantage of longitudinal data collection is the ability to track transitions and outcomes after the initial interview. Participation in the firm creation process involves several important transitions. The first is identifying entry into the process. In many cases this decision

---

[4]Students living at home or off campus would be eligible and are included in the cohort.

[5]The lack of information about activities before the first interview is defined as the left truncation problem; lack of information about the status or outcomes after the last interview is considered the right truncation problem. A variety of strategies have developed to deal with the left truncation problem based on data collected in the first interview about previous activities.

or commitment may emerge over time. This is similar to two people that may gradually realize that they should marry. They may, however, announce a firm date of an engagement, a public commitment to enter the "marriage planning" process. There will be, in all cases, a precise date when a marriage contract is "executed." Precise descriptions of the firm creation process are facilitated by precise criteria for defining the date of entry into the start-up process and when outcomes, such as profitable operations, occur.

Precisely defined, widely accepted criteria for dating the early stages of the firm life course do not exist. Most critical is estimating date of entry into the firm creation process, as the initial screening interviews identify those active at an arbitrary point in the process. Some may have been involved for weeks and others for years. Obtaining the dates for initiating a range of activities in the initial interview has led to a variety of strategies for defining the date of entry into the process. This has included the date of the screening interview, first activity initiated, and date of initial serious thought, or when the business idea developed.[6] One assessment utilized the first activity after initial serious thought.[7] This criterion would shift date of entry for that 26% of the cases that initiated activity before serious thought to a later date, treat that 32% that report serious thought and an activity in the same month as an entry date, and delay the date for the 41% that report an activity one or more months after serious thought.[8]

Given that many potential nascent entrepreneurs think about—and talk about—starting a business than actually pursue firm creation, another strategy is to ignore reports of "initial serious thought" and focus on reports of behavior, implementation of start-up activities. Assuming that a minimal level of intensity would be an indicator of seriousness of intent, the first of any two activities implemented within twelve months provides a firm date for entry into business creation. With this criterion, used in the following assessment, serious thought is reported prior to

---

[6]Summary in Reynolds and Curtin (2009) and Tornikoski and Renko (2014).

[7]Yang and Aldrich (2012).

[8]Based on the patterns in 3,212 unweighted cases in four cohorts in three countries in the consolidated file discussed below, omitting Sweden due to absence of data on serious thought in the first three waves of data collection.

the date of entry for 53% of the cases, in the same month for 28%, and after date of entry for 19%. For 1% of the cases serious thought occurs 4 or more years after the data of entry.[9]

While the PSED procedure, screening for active nascent entrepreneurs followed by details about current efforts, does provide a representative sample, it also leads to a potential complication. Those that take a long time to implement a new firm are more likely to be identified as active nascent entrepreneurs and included in the data set. There may be an underrepresentation of those that move quickly to implement a new firm. One solution has been to eliminate cases with an entry date well before the initial screening interview, such as cases that entered the process in the previous 9 months[10] or two years;[11] either strategy leads to a substantial loss of cases. Excluding those cases with a start date 120 months (ten years) before the first interview eliminates the extreme "long in process cases" but retains most of the sample.[12]

There are two other transitions to be "dated." One is a shift from a start-up to a new firm and the other is disengagement from the start-up effort. While these transitions may also reflect an adjustment period—it may take a while for the principals to realize a change in the situation—a specific date is required for precise assessments. For the following analysis a new firm birth is considered to have occurred with the monthly revenue is greater than all monthly expenses including the payments to the owner-managers.[13] Disengagement is assumed when

---

[9]Based on 2,947 unweighted cases in three countries in the consolidated file discussed below, omitting Sweden due to absence of dates on serious though in the first three waves of data collection.

[10]Delmar and Shane (2003).

[11]Liao and Gartner (2006);

[12]Among 3,639 cases in the five cohort data set, 1.6% have an entry date ten years prior to the initial wave 1 detailed interview, 5.0% five to ten years prior, 8.5% three to five years prior, 73.2% up to 2 years prior, and 1.6% after the wave 1 interview. These latter cases qualified for entry on the basis of start-up activities initiated after the wave 1 interview.

[13]Three other criteria are widely used to defined "firm birth" such as a major time commitment by the principal(s) to the start-up effort, registration of the nascent venture in an administrative data set, and the first economic transaction (purchase or sale) implemented on behalf of the new firm. These alternative definitions have a major impact on the description and interpretation of the firm creation process

no member of the start-up team is devoting any time to the implementation of that business.

There will be a focus on three features of the firm creation process.

- What proportions of start-up initiatives lead to different outcomes?

- How long does it take after entry into business creation before an outcome occurs?

- What is the relationship between start-up activities and these outcomes?

While simple to describe, answers to these questions are complicated to develop. There are a large number of potential activities, most individual cases of business creation involves a unique set of activities, and every possible sequence of activities are found among start-up efforts.

The second focus is on how the activities pursued in business creation are related to the outcomes. This is related to both the actual outcomes—initial profits or disengagement—as well the time required to reach an outcome. It is generally better for all concerned if the start-up effort can achieve profits or disengage sooner rather than later.

---

and are discussed elsewhere (Schoonhoven, Burton, and Reynolds, 2009; Reynolds, 2015a).

5

Overview of the Business Start-up Process

Six years after entry into the start-up process, about one in three nascent ventures (34%) have reached initial profits, almost half (44%) have quit, and about one in five (22%) are still in the start-up mode.[1] These transitions are presented for over two thousand cases from four countries in Figure 5.1. The outcome proportions are presented for each three month period following entry into business creation, where 100% are considered to be active in the start-up process. As can be seen in Figure 2, the proportions that reach initial profits or disengage changes gradually over time.

There is considerable difference among countries – or entrepreneurial ecology – on the proportion reaching initial profits. After 72 months it is greatest for urban China (54%) and least for the national cohorts from the U.S. (24% and 32%), with intermediate values for Sweden (42%) and Australia (33%). These differences are summarized

---

[1] A project tracking 290 Austrian nascent entrepreneurs found that 55% starting businesses three years after contacting various agencies and programs for assistance. As these ventures were not identified at the time of entry into the process those that had disengaged before seeking assistance were not included in the cohort (Kessler and Frank, 2009).

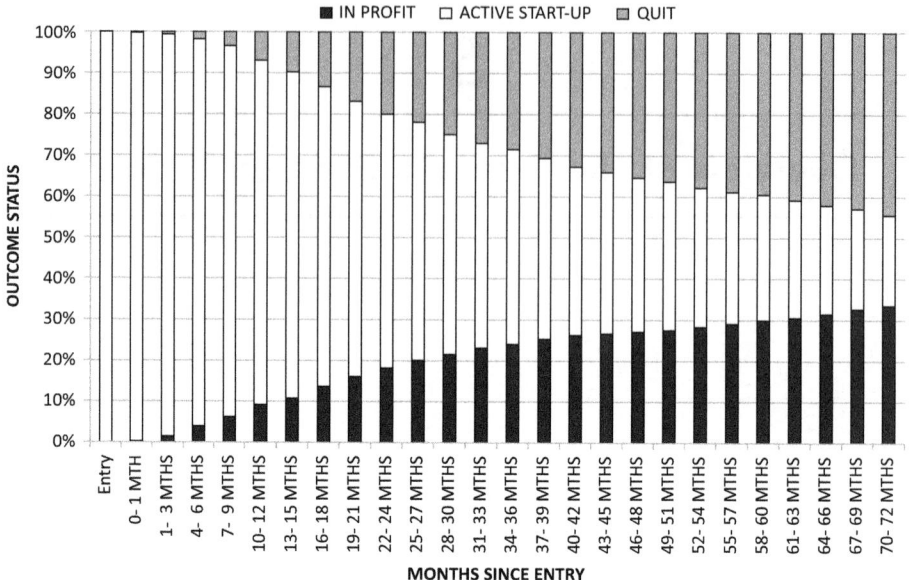

Figure 5.1: Outcome Status by Months since Entry.[2]

at 72 months in Table 5.1 and the patterns to achieve profitability over time in Figure 5.2.

The high proportion of Chinese start-ups that reach profits may reflect some distinctive features. There were only two follow-ups and the second, 24 month survey, had a low response rate. Many start-ups that had discontinued may not have been reached for a follow-up. Further, the cohort was identified in 2009, just when the Chinese economy was growing rapidly; high levels of demand may have facilitated firm profitability. The other national differences, reflecting more follow-ups and higher response rates, may be more reliable. There is more success in Australia and Sweden than the U.S.

Start-up efforts abandoned at 72 months also varies among countries, also presented in Table 5.1 and in Figure 5.3. This varies from 32%

---

[2]Based on all cases from five cohorts considered active nascent entrepreneurs that have entered the process; there is outcome data on 2,513 cases at entry which declines over time to 2,059 cases after 72 months.

Table 5.1: Start-up Outcomes by Cohort.

	Outcome at 72 months			Mean time (mths):		
	Profit	Active	Quit	To profit	Still active	To quit
Australia	33.2%	34.3%	32.5%	26.8	41.6	22.0
China	54.4%	3.7%	41.9%	18.7	30.3	18.2
Sweden	41.8%	20.0%	38.2%	17.9	62.4	28.7
US PSED I	32.0%	30.3%	37.7%	37.7	82.4	34.4
US PSED II	24.3%	17.1%	58.6%	28.4	92.4	33.1
All cohorts	33.5%	22.0%	44.5%	26.4	58.3	29.8

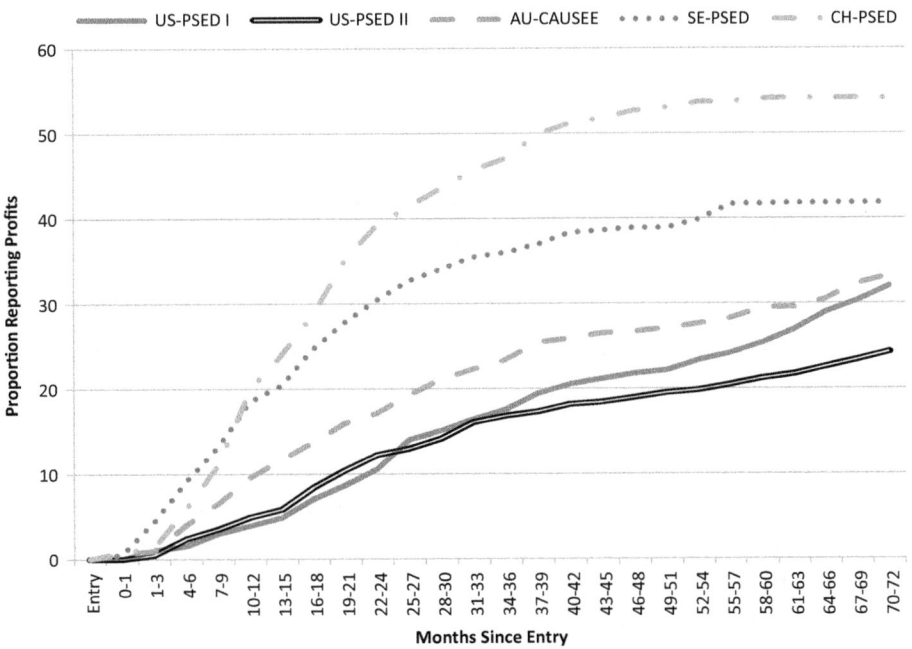

Figure 5.2: Proportion Reporting Profits by Months after Entry by Cohort.

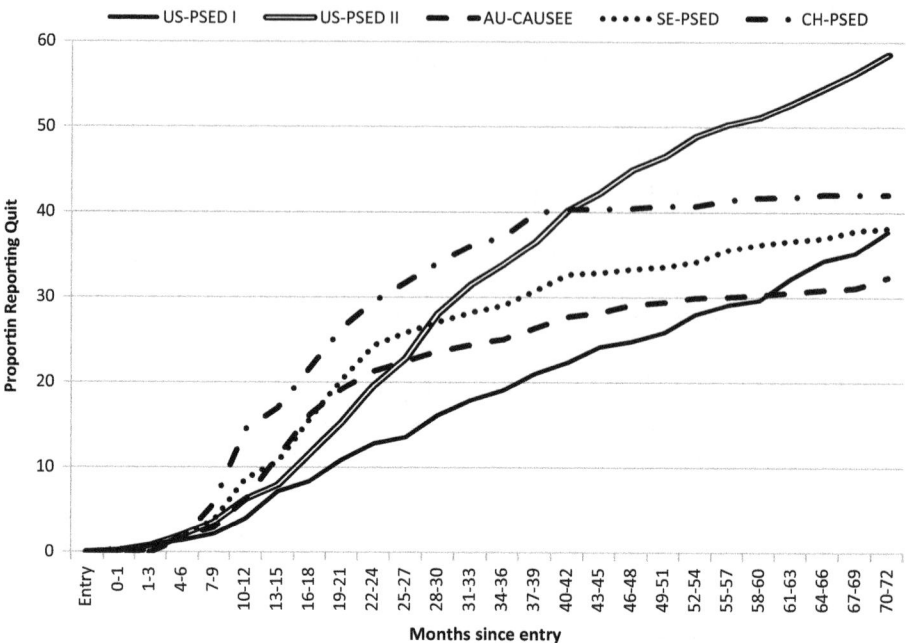

Figure 5.3: Proportion Reporting Quitting by Months after Entry by Cohort.

for Australia to 59% for the US PSED II cohort. China, Sweden, and the US PSED I cohort are within this range. This diversity is reflected in the third option, actively engaged with the start-up 72 months after entry. This varied from 4% for China to 34% for Australia; the US cohorts are intermediate at 17% and 30%. The Swedish cohort is almost average at 20%.

Overall, the average time to reach profits (26 months) is slightly shorter than the average time to quit (30 months). Again, there is variation among countries. As shown in Table 5.1, the average time to reach profits in China and Sweden, about 18 months, is much shorter than for Australia (27 months) or U.S. PSED II (28 months). US PSED I is the longest at 38 months. Except for China, the times to abandon a project tend to be longer; there is less variation among the other four cohorts. The average times of those still in the start-up process are the longest, averaging 58 months or almost six years. These national averages are shortest in Australia and China, but may reflect differences in the nature and number of the follow-up interviews. Extended periods of activity without a resolution are longest in the United States, with averages of seven to eight years.

Variation in the time required to reach an outcome is reflected in the variation in the slope of the curves during the first 36 months in Figure 5.2 for initial profits and Figure 5.3 for disengagement. Steeper curves in the early months are represented by a shorter average time to outcome. On the other hand, there are cases in all countries of very long times required to reach an outcome.

While there is variation among countries in both the proportion of start-ups that reach profitability and the amount of time required to reach an outcome, the variation within countries is much greater. This leads directly to two issues

- Is there some systematic relationship between the activities pursued in the business creation process and the outcomes?

- Is there some systematic relationship between the activities pursued in the business creation process and the time to reach an outcome?

This is the focus of the following assessment.

5.1 Prevalence of Start-up Activities

A multitude of activities can be involved in developing and implementing a new business. Individuals and teams working on start-ups pursue a wide range of activities. The mix can vary dramatically based on the nature of the products or services, stage in the start-up process, and resources available to the business. There may also be variation in the time pressure; some nascent ventures may be implemented at a leisurely pace and others under considerable time pressure from competitors or those providing resources, such as outside investors. An inventory of the most common activities and the timing of their implementation would do much to clarify what occurs in the start-up process.

Nineteen start-up activities could be harmonized across the five cohorts. They are listed along with the actual interview items in Table 5.2.

Table 5.2: Start-up Activities Interview Items.

Start-up Activity	Interview item
Serious thought	Have you spent a lot of time thinking about this new business?
Invest own money	Have you invested any of your own money in this business?
Began business plan	Has a business plan been prepared for this start-up?
Define markets	Has an effort been made to define the market opportunities by talking with potential customers or getting information about the competition?
Develop model, prototype	Has there been work on developing a model or prototype for delivery of the product or service?
Financial projections	Have projected financial statements, such as income and cash flow statements, been developed/
Purchased materials, supplies, parts	Have any raw materials, inventory, supplies or components been purchased/
Promote products or services	Have marketing or promotional efforts been started for the products or services this start-up will be selling/
Leased, acquired major assets	Have any major items equipment, facilities or property been purchased, leased, or rented for the new start-up?
Sales, income, or revenue	Has the new business received any money, income or fees from the sale of goods or services/

(*Continued*)

Table 5.2: (*Continued*)

Start-up Activity	Interview item
Phone book, website listing	Does the new business have its own phone or website listing? [The website option was added after the year 2000.]
Supplier credit	Has credit with a supplier been established?
Full time work on the start-up	Have you (the respondent or team member one) begun to devote full time to the business—35 or more hours per week?
Organized start-up team	Has a start-up team been organized?
Acquired registration number	Has this new business be registered with the appropriate government agency? [As procedures are different in each country, this question is modified for each national context.]
Hired employees	Have any employees or managers been hired for pay—workers that would not share ownership?
Asked for external funds	Have financial institutions or other people been asked for funds?
Patent, copyright, trademark filing	Has an application for a patent, copyright, or trademark relevant to this new business been submitted?
Got external funding	Have you received the first outside finding from financial institutions or other people for this new business?

Note: As the actual questions differed somewhat between projects and different languages, such as English, Chinese and Swedish, this presentation reflects the core activities associated with each item.

This is, however, less than a third of the 66 different start-up activities tracked in one or more projects. (The U.S.PSED II data set includes 51 start-up activities.)[3] Occurrence reflected a positive response to the items listed in Table 5.3, indicating that the activity has been initiated. Some, such as developing a business plan, may take some time to complete. The order of the questions varied from project to project and these specific items were often intermingled with items about other start-up activities. There are many situations where a particular activity is not relevant to the venture being implemented. Only a minority, for example, would find it useful to pursue legal ownership of intellectual property, such as a patent, trademark, or copyright.

However, these activities cover all the major domains considered important in business creation, including those involving customers, suppliers, employees, financial sponsors, government agencies, assembling a start-up team, hiring employees, and the like. In some cases they may be considered indicators of a broader range of interrelated activities associated with business creation.

Most significant, if a respondent reports that any of these activities have been initiated, they are asked the month and year in which this activity first occurred. This information is the basis for creating a start-up time line for each case of business creation. As a consequence, these case specific time lines are unrelated to the actual dates when the interviews were completed. This is a major benefit in the following assessments.

The prevalence of these 19 activities for all cases in each cohort is presented in Table 5.3. They are rank ordered by the average prevalence rate for the five cohorts. The response to "Have you given serious thought to this effort?" is virtually universal for four cohorts. It is lower for Sweden (42%) because it was not asked until the fourth interview; so many Swedish nascent entrepreneurs may have disengaged or reached initial profits before having an opportunity to respond.[4] Because it is

---

[3] An initial list was developed for an assessment with a convenience sample over twenty years ago (Gatewood, Shaver, and Gartner, 1995). Expansion for the US PSED I project was a collaborative effort and other PSED projects have made adjustments (Gartner, Carter, and Reynolds, 2004).

[4] The presence of Swedish cases without this information posed a dilemma for the

Table 5.3: Prevalence of Start-up Activities by Cohort.

VARIABLE NAME	START-UP ACTIVITY	US-PSED I	US-PSED II	AU-CAUSEE	SE-PSED	CH-PSED	PROJ AVG
Number of cases		673	909	519	407	408	
PROPORTION RESPONDING							
THINK_AW	Serious thought	100.0	99.2	99.4	42.0	100.0	88.1
ONINVAW1	Invest own money	96.4	87.9	93.3	72.1	78.2	85.6
DFNMKTAW	Define markets	95.0	72.1	81.2	75.4	82.8	81.3
BUSPLNAW	Began business plan	71.4	79.3	76.1	94.7	81.0	80.5
MODEL_AW	Developed model, prototype	89.3	81.5	70.5	72.1	40.2	70.7
PURCHAAW	Purchased materials, supplies, parts	83.7	78.9	76.2	53.5	57.2	69.9
FINPRJAW	Financial projections	58.3	53.2	60.7	84.6	85.7	68.5

(*Continued*)

Table 5.3: (*Continued*)

VARIABLE NAME	START-UP ACTIVITY	US-PSED I	US-PSED II	AU-CAUSEE	SE-PSED	CH-PSED	PROJ AVG
PROMOTAW	Promote products or services	75.6	68.5	69.4	61.3	46.2	64.2
LEASE_AW	Leased, acquired major assets	69.3	72.4	67.5	55.3	52.7	63.4
SALES_AW	Sales, income, or revenue	65.8	74.9	65.7	68.3	34.9	61.9
PHLISTAW	Phone book listing for firm	29.7	71.3	81.9	42.2	23.9	49.8
SUPCRDAW	Obtaining supplied credit	55.5	43.4	34.6	35.7	74.1	48.7
FTWK_AW1	Full time work on start-up work	51.4	32.6	42.6	46.0	65.1	47.5
BUSREGAW	Acquired registration number	51.5	40.1	10.6	60.6	29.6	38.5

(*Continued*)

Table 5.3: (*Continued*)

VARIABLE NAME	START-UP ACTIVITY	US-PSED I	US-PSED II	AU-CAUSEE	SE-PSED	CH-PSED	PROJ AVG
SUTEAMAW	Began to organized start-up team	60.6	9.8	16.1	50.8	28.6	33.2
HIRE__AW	Hired employee	28.3	25.8	21.4	28.3	47.8	30.3
ASKFNDAW	Asked for formal funding	35.2	31.2	*6.9	35.8	26.3	27.1
PATENTAW	Patent, copyright, trademark filing	27.0	11.5	1.7	20.1	13.7	14.8
GETFNDAW	Got initial formal financing	13.4	23.6	12.8	16.5	10.2	15.3

Based on those cases identified as active nascent entrepreneurs adjusted with population and venture size weights, n = 2,916. Includes activities identified in any interview wave. Project average is the average across the five cohorts. Some cases only completed the first detailed interview.

*If the respondent cannot provide at least the year the activity was initiated, the activity is treated as a missing value in the data set. This would account for a lower proportion identified as asking for funding than reporting receipt of funding, where a date is provided.

universal and may not require much of a personal commitment, "serious thought" is not used to define the date of entry into the start-up process.

Aside from serious thought, all 18 other activities involved some behavioral effort on the part of the nascent entrepreneur. There is some consistency across the five cohorts, with owner investment of personal funds in the business, defining markets, and developing a business plan reported by a strong majority. At the other extreme a minority report asking others for funding, pursuing intellectual property rights (patents, trademarks, or copyrights) or receiving financial support from other investors or a financial institution.

In addition to the initiation of these activities, their timing in the firm creation process may be critical. The average prevalence and time after entry into the start-up process are presented for all cases with outcome data in Figure 5.4. The light colored bars above the horizontal axis represent the proportion that reported each start-up activity and the dark bars, above and below the axis, represent the number of months when the activity occurred after entry into the start-up process. The acts are arranged in terms of average time after entry into the start-up process. The final outcome, initial profits or disengagement, are to the far right of Figure 5.4.

As serious thought was not used to determine the entry date, it is of no surprise that it occurs, on average, 18 months prior to entry. But five activities reported by 80% of the start-ups seem to occur, on average, within the first year: development of a model or prototype for delivery to a customer, defining the potential market, development of a business plan, investment of the entrepreneur's own money, and acquiring supplies, parts, inventories, components, etc.

The other 13 start-up activities are reported by a smaller proportion of the cohort and take longer to implement. Less than 18% report

---

analysis. It did not affect the identification of the date of entry, as "serious thought" was not one of the start-up activities included in this assessment. Given a choice of omitting the Swedish cohort and pursing analysis with the Swedish cohort knowing that missing data may affect the outcome the latter strategy was adopted. There is no evidence that it made a major difference.

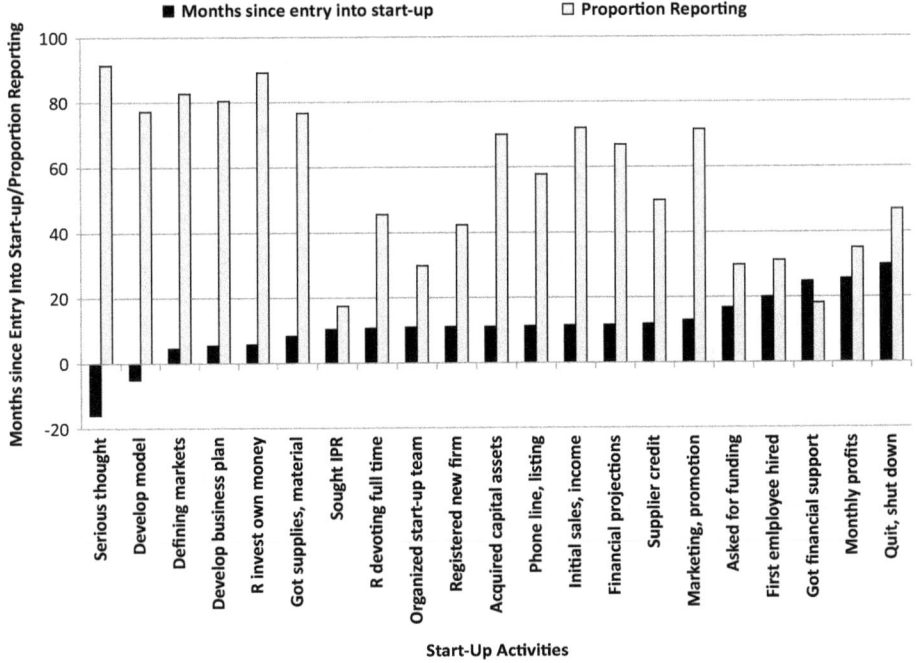

Figure 5.4: Start-up Acts, Lag from Entry and Prevalence.[5]

efforts to obtain copyrights, patents, or trademarks (intellectual property rights) and it takes a year after entry into the process. Fulltime effort by a potential owner occurs after about a year for 40% of the cases, followed by that 25% that report organizing a start-up team. Other activities reported by a majority of the new ventures and occurring 12-18 months after entry include acquiring capital assets, obtaining a phone book or website listing, initial sales or income, creating financial projections, obtaining supplier credit, and initiating marketing or promotions. About two in five report registering the firm in slightly less than a year after entry. Much later in the process, after 18 months, 25% report seeking outside financial support and after 20 months 25% have hired an employee. On average, obtaining outside funding occurs

---

[5]All start-ups with 72 month follow data using venture weights adjustment, n = 2,051.

after 24 months for less than 20% of the ventures.

As shown in Figure 5.4, and consistent with the bottom row of Table 5.1, about 34% report initial profits after 26 months and 44% disengagement after 30 months. The remaining 22% are still active in the start-up process after 72 months.

5.2   Amount of Start-up Activity and Outcomes

There is considerable variation in both the number and speed with which start-up activities are initiated in the first six years after entry into the start-up process. This diversity is presented in Table 5.4, which indicates the number of activities initiated in the first, three, six, twelve and twenty-four months after entry into the start-up process. While the typical nascent venture gradually increases the range of start-up activity over the first two years, a number of nascent ventures have a high level of activity soon after entry into the process. A small number of cases, less than 1%, report 10 or more activities in the first month; by 24 months 36% have initiated 10 more activities.

Table 5.4: Diversity in Start-up Activity 1, 3, 6, 12, and 24 Months after Entry.

	0-1 Mth	0-3 Mths	0-6 Mths	0-12 Mths	0-24 Mths
Average number	2.1	3.3	4.7	6.6	8.1
Up to 3 activities	84.8%	64.6%	45.5%	20.9%	9.5%
4 or 5 activities	9.9%	16.2%	18.9%	21.3%	15.6%
6 or 7 activities	3.3%	10.9%	15.7%	19.5%	19.4%
8 or 9 activities	1.4%	4.7%	11.1%	18.5%	19.5%
10 or 11 activities	0.6%	2.6%	5.2%	11.0%	18.6%
12 to 18 activities	0.1%	1.0%	3.6%	8.9%	17.4%
	100.0%	100.0%	100.0%	100.0%	100.0%

The relationship between the culmination of activities over time and the outcomes is presented in Figure 5.5. The cumulative count of activities in the first six months is very similar for the profitable and disengaged ventures. The major differences between those in profit and disengaged occurs between 6 and 24 months after entry. After 24

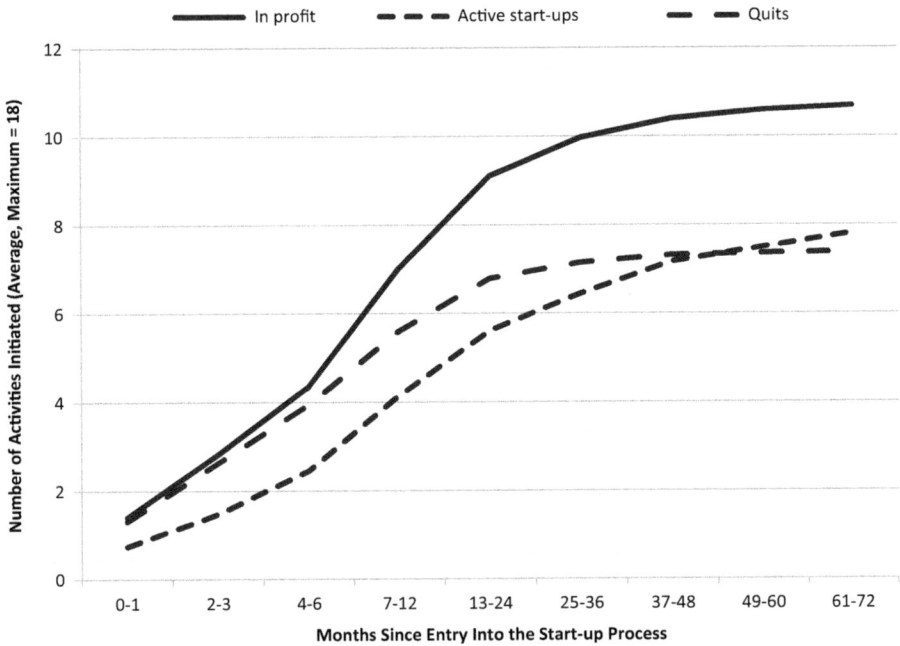

Figure 5.5: Start-up Activities over Time by Outcome.[6]

months those that disengaged have a level of activity similar to those still active in the start-up process. After 48 months those still active report a slight increase in start-up activities, slightly more than those that quit after 60 months.

Those that are still active in the start-up process after 72 months have a distinctive pattern; their level of activity is significantly lower from the very first month they enter into the start-up process. As shown in Figure 5.5, their level of activity remains much lower than those achieving profitability over the entire 72 months and lower than those that quit for the first 36 months or three years. After 48 months, or four years, they report slightly more activity than those that quit. There is no question that for whatever reason—lack of skill or preparation for business creation, inability to assemble resources, ambiguity about

---

[6]Start-ups with outcome data at 72 months, venture weights, n = 2,059.

the business idea—those tentatively exploring business creation have a quite different record of involvement.

Overall, the major patterns associated with the number and speed of implementing start-up activities suggest:

- Those reporting more activities are more likely to reach initial profits.

- Those reporting more activities in the first six months are more likely to reach initial profits or disengage.

- Those reporting fewer activities in the first 12 months are more likely to continue as active in the start-up process.

Attention to the impact of specific activities may improve the predictive accuracy and provide more detail about the processes associated with different outcomes.

5.3 Specific Start-up Activities and Outcomes

It is clear that the amount of start-up activity is related to subsequent outcomes. Those cases that eventually reach initial profits have more activity in the first several years than those disengaging or continuing in the start-up process. But some specific activity may have greater association with outcomes than others.

This can be explored by considering the association of each activity reported in the first 72 months with the different outcomes. This is provided for all activities in Table 5.5. The activities are rank ordered in terms of the difference between those in profit or discontinued after 72 months. Because of the large sample size, virtually all differences are statistically significant.

The largest difference is associated with initial sales. While virtually all cases reaching initial profits report initial sales, it is only fifty percent of those that discontinue. There are differences of 27% to 35% for hiring employees, registration of the start-up venture, and the respondent devoting full time to the effort, acquiring capital assets, and obtaining supplier credit. At the other extreme, the differences are 6% or less

Table 5.5: Start-up Activities: Proportion Initiated by Outcome.

Start-up Activity Initiated in first 72 months	In profit	Active Start-up	Quit Quit	Difference: Profit-Quits	Stat sign
Initial sales, income*	98.4	76.0	49.9	48.5	0.000
First employee hired	53.3	24.5	17.9	35.3	0.000
Registered new firm	60.5	40.6	29.4	31.1	0.000
R devoting full time	63.4	43.8	32.9	30.5	0.000
Acquired capital assets	84.7	75.7	56.1	28.6	0.000
Supplier credit	66.6	44.7	39.6	26.9	0.000
Phone line, listing	69.2	60.3	48.0	21.2	0.000
Marketing, promotion	83.3	70.3	63.0	20.3	0.000
Financial projections	80.1	59.5	60.5	19.6	0.000
Got supplies, material	85.7	79.8	68.1	17.6	0.000
Organized start-up team	38.8	29.7	22.9	15.9	0.000
Got financial support	25.9	19.1	11.8	14.1	0.000
Asked for funding	35.6	26.2	27.2	8.3	0.000
R invest own money	92.7	92.6	84.8	8.0	0.000
Sought IPR	21.9	17.6	14.0	7.9	0.000
Serious thought	95.1	94.5	87.3	7.8	0.000
Defining markets	85.8	83.6	79.9	6.0	0.006
Develop business plan	83.7	79.3	78.4	5.3	0.026
Develop model	78.5	82.1	73.6	4.9	0.001

*If the date of initiation was not provided, the activity is treated as a missing value, which would reduce proportion of valid cases reporting sales for those in profit in first 72 months.

for activities reported by three in four of the start-up efforts, such as developing a model for delivery of the product or service, development of a business plan, defining the potential markets, or giving serious thought to the new venture.

Table 5.6: Start-up Activities: Time to Initiation (Months) and Outcome.

Start-up Activity Initiated in First 72 Months	In profit	Active Start-up	Quit	Difference: Profit-Quits	Stat sign
Sought IPR	12.9	18.4	2.5	10.4	0.044
Got financial support	21.1	45.2	14.4	6.7	0.000
First employee hired	18.3	35.4	13.4	5.0	0.000
Asked for funding	14.8	31.2	10.3	4.6	0.000
Supplier credit	11.3	21.6	6.9	4.3	0.000
Initial sales, income	10.5	19.5	6.6	3.9	0.000
Phone line, listing	10.1	20.6	6.7	3.3	0.000
Acquired capital assets	10.5	17.8	7.2	3.3	0.000
R devoting full time	9.1	21.3	6.1	3.0	0.000
Marketing, promotion	11.9	21.4	9.0	2.9	0.000
Got supplies, material	7.7	15.2	4.9	2.8	0.000
Organized start-up team	9.4	20.5	6.6	2.7	0.000
Defining markets	3.3	13.0	1.0	2.3	0.000
Develop business plan	4.3	13.1	2.5	1.8	0.000
Financial projections	9.4	23.8	7.7	1.7	0.000
R invest own money	4.9	11.4	3.5	1.4	0.000
Registered new firm	9.7	16.8	9.1	0.7	0.005
Serious thought	−15.2	−29.2	−14.3	−1.0	0.069
Develop model	−5.7	−0.4	−0.7	−5.0	0.171

The average time after entry into the start-up process before the activity is initiated is presented in relation to outcomes in Table 5.6. These are also rank ordered by the difference between those that report profits by 72 months and those start-up efforts ventures that were terminated. In almost all cases, however, the time lag is greatest for those ventures still in the start-up process after 72 months, reflecting a more tenuous involvement in business creation. Further, they reported serious though much earlier, by over a year, than those achieving initial profit or disengagement.

The most striking feature of the comparison is that for every statistically significant difference, those cases that were disengaged by 72 months initiated activity sooner than those in profit at 72 months. The differences for the exceptions, initial serious thought and development of a model or a prototype, are not statistically significant. The differences are systematic; those that have disengaged by 72 months were quicker to initiate start-up activities compared to those that achieved initial profits. This suggests they were committed to testing the viability of their business venture as quickly as possible.

In summary, there are two dramatic differences between those cases reporting profits and those that were shut down after 72 months:

- Those that quit were less likely to initiate any start-up activity.

- Those that quit initiated activities sooner than those that reported initial profits.

This would suggest nascent teams quickly implementing start-up activities discovered that the venture might not be viable and discontinued their efforts.

Those that reached profitability and quit were equally likely to have worked on a business plan. But those that quit did so in the first two and a half months, or 10 weeks, much sooner than the 4.3 months, or 17 weeks, for those that reached initial profits. This is a difference of almost two months. Initiating a business plan appears to have facilitated a decision to disengage from the start-up effort. This may have reduced the sunk costs, time and money, invested in a venture that was not to become profitable.

6

Initiating Start-up Activities and Outcomes

While reviewing the average prevalence and timing of start-up activities helps provide an overview of the process, there is considerable diversity among the cases. Many engage in a great deal of activity early in the process. Table 6.1 presents the start-up activities reported by the end of the 1, 3, 6, 12, and 24 month in the start-up process. They are rank ordered by prevalence in the first month.

There are several important features presented in Table 6.1. Every activity has been reported as occurring in the first month by more than one start-up initiative. *There is no one way to begin the business creation process.* The activities mentioned by the largest proportion is developing a model for providing the good or service and working on a business plan, both reported by more than a third of the cases.

Second, the rank order of activities is relatively stable; those receiving the most attention in the first month are about the same as after 24 months. One exception is the proportion of owners that have invested funds in the start-up increased from 28% to 82%, moving it from fourth in the first month to first after 24 months, but other activities have about the same rank order.

Table 6.1: Start-up Activities 1, 3, 6, 12 and 24 Months after Entry.

Activity	1st month	Up to 3 months	Up to 6 months	Up to 12 months	Up to 24 months
Serious thought	74.8%	79.0%	84.0%	88.2%	88.2%
Develop model	37.2%	45.8%	55.7%	66.6%	72.9%
Develop business plan	35.6%	44.2%	53.0%	64.8%	72.4%
Defining markets	31.1%	41.8%	50.9%	65.0%	74.1%
R invest own money	27.6%	40.7%	53.3%	70.9%	81.8%
Got supplies, material	16.9%	27.5%	40.2%	57.6%	68.0%
Financial projections	15.5%	23.5%	32.5%	46.7%	57.0%
Acquired capital assets	13.3%	21.8%	31.8%	47.4%	58.8%
Initial sales, income	11.6%	22.0%	32.2%	47.2%	60.8%
Marketing, promotion	11.3%	19.8%	30.0%	45.8%	59.5%
Phone line, listing	11.2%	19.2%	27.5%	39.3%	49.6%
R devoting full time	9.1%	15.1%	20.1%	31.0%	38.8%
Supplier credit	8.5%	14.1%	20.6%	32.1%	41.0%
Organized start-up team	7.9%	11.8%	14.8%	19.9%	24.4%
Registered new firm	7.4%	11.3%	16.2%	25.3%	34.9%
Asked for funding	4.6%	7.6%	11.4%	17.1%	22.2%
Sought IPR	2.7%	4.1%	6.2%	9.9%	13.5%
First employee hired	2.5%	4.7%	8.2%	14.6%	21.8%
Got financial support	1.1%	2.1%	3.7%	7.5%	11.8%
Average/Start-up venture	2.55	3.77	5.08	7.09	8.63

It is possible that implementing some activities early in the process may be related to the outcomes after 72 months. Those activities with a statistically significant relationship after one month and six months are presented in Table 6.2.

There are some interesting associations. About 52% of those nascent ventures that hire in the first month are in profit by 72 months, compared to the 33% of all cases. Other activities associated with initial profits include organizing a start-up team, devoting full time work to the initiative, and developing financial projections. Some activities, however, seem to be associated with other outcomes. Compared to 22% of all cases, 36% of the cases that report sales or income in the first month are still in the start-up phase after 72 months. And while 44%

Table 6.2: First, Sixth Month Start-up Activities and Outcomes.

	Initiated in first month				Initiated in first six months			
	Profits	SU Active	Quit	Stat Sign	Profits	SU Active	Quit	Stat Sign
72 Month Outcome	33.5%	22.1%	44.4%		33.5%	22.1%	44.4%	
Hired Employee	52.9%	17.6%	29.4%	0.011	51.5%	11.2%	37.3%	0.000
Start-up Team	45.4%	16.0%	38.7%	0.003	44.7%	15.1%	40.1%	0.000
Full time Work	44.4%	20.9%	34.8%	0.003	44.3%	15.7%	40.0%	0.000
Business Registration					42.9%	20.4%	36.6%	0.000
Financial Projections	44.2%	12.8%	45.0%	0.000	42.9%	12.6%	44.5%	0.000
Supplier Credit					41.7%	13.9%	44.5%	0.000
Sales, Income	37.2%	36.4%	26.4%	0.025	38.8%	19.8%	41.5%	0.002
Capital assets					38.5%	19.3%	42.2%	0.003
Define Markets	38.1%	16.4%	45.4%	0.000	37.3%	15.8%	46.9%	0.000
Promote output	37.1%	15.9%	47.0%	0.055	37.3%	15.4%	47.3%	0.000
Phone, Internet					36.7%	18.6%	44.7%	0.032
Business Plan	34.2%	18.7%	47.1%	0.022	35.3%	18.0%	46.6%	0.000
Asked for Funding					35.0%	10.3%	54.7%	0.000
Serious Thought	34.5%	20.9%	44.6%	0.063	34.5%	21.0%	44.5%	0.016
Personal Investment					34.1%	18.7%	47.2%	0.000

of all nascent ventures have been abandoned after 72 months, it is 47% of those that are developing business plans in the first month.

Considering the activities initiated in the first six months after entry into the start-up process, fifteen of nineteen have a statistically significant relationship to the outcome, as presented in Table 6.2. Nascent ventures that have achieved initial profits are more likely to have initiated any of these fifteen.

The focus on specific activities implemented early in the process tends to distract from two critical features of the association with outcomes. First, those that achieve profits have generally implemented more activities, as show in Figure 5.5. Second, after several years virtually all activities have a statistically significant relationship to the outcome, as presented below in Table 7.1, which presents the relationship of activities implemented in the first 24 months. Determining which of the activities are the most critical to affecting the outcomes requires a different strategy.

7

Assessing Relative Impact of Start-up Activities

In addition to start-up activities, a number of other factors may have an impact on the outcomes. Such as the national context, economic sector, nature of the business venture, and the background of those involved in starting the business.

The effect of the national context, shown in Figures 3 and 4, differs for Australia, China, Sweden and the United States. The economic sector in which the new venture will compete may affect the outcomes. These are best considered nominal factors, where a different impact may be expected but the characteristics that are the basis for the variation have not been identified. Why there are more profitable start-ups in China than the United States has not been determined.

It would be convenient to characterize nascent entrepreneur age and educational attainment by a simple interval variable, such as the number of years. This practice assumes a linear effect of these factors, more is assumed to increase or decrease the outcome. However, prior research indicates a more complicated relationship. For example, it is well documented that participation in business creation is highest among those 25-35 years old, much lower for those 18-24 or over 55 years old. Clearly, this is an inverted U-shaped pattern, not a simple linear relationship.

Similar issues may arise with regard to educational attainment. While in developed countries, participation in business creation appears to be rather low among those with little education, it increases as a step function among those that have completed secondary education (high school). In contrast, in developing countries, where there are more limited job opportunities, participation in business creation is often higher among those with little education.[1]

There are, then, four independent variables where a linear relationship to the outcomes cannot be assumed. They are the host country, economic sector, age, and educational attainment. In all cases dichotomous (or dummy) variables are created, each reflecting a different status on the variable. For all four variables one status is omitted from the regression analysis, to provide a basis for comparison of the other statuses. The base statuses are the United States, the extractive sector, a primary team member that is 18-24 years old, and education up to a high school degree.

The unilateral effect of the independent factors on the outcomes at 72 months after entry into the start-ups process is presented in Table 7.1. The impact on the time required to reach the outcome is provided in Table 7.2. In both cases, the independent variables reflect activities in the first 24 months of the start-up process and the outcome measures are identified in the 72 months after entry into the start-up process. A start-up venture may have been identified as profitable or abandoned at any time from the first to the seventy-second month.

Almost every variable in Table 7.1 has, taken by itself, a statistically significant impact on reports of profitability or disengagement 72 months after entry into the process. The major exceptions being the gender of team member one (or the respondent), the extent of experience with or business start-ups, the size of the start-up team, formation of a start-up team, and initiation of serious thought—which

---

[1]Reviewed in some detail in an assessment of the business creation among the bottom billions (Reynolds, 2012).

Table 7.1: Independent Variables and Outcomes.

		New Firm	Active	Quit	StatSign
	Outcome reported	33.5%	22.1%	44.5%	
COUNTRY	Australia	33.2%	34.3%	32.5%	
	China	54.4%	3.7%	41.9%	
	Sweden	41.8%	20.0%	38.2%	
	United States	27.1%	22.0%	50.8%	0.000
TM1_SEX	Male	33.9%	23.3%	42.8%	
	Female	33.0%	22.2%	46.8%	0.129
TM1_AGE_6C	Team mbr 1: 18-24 yrs old	38.2%	8.9%	52.8%	
	Team mbr 1: 25-34 yrs old	34.0%	21.3%	44.7%	
	Team mbr 1: 35-44 yrs old	34.9%	23.5%	41.6%	
	Team mbr 1: 45-54 yrs old	31.8%	23.1%	45.1%	
	Team mbr 1: 55-64 yrs old	29.3%	34.7%	35.9%	
	Team mbr 1: 65-up yrs old	17.6%	26.5%	55.9%	0.000
TM1_EDUC	Team mbr 1: Up to high school	34.9%	19.1%	46.0%	
	Team mbr 1: Post HS, pre coll	34.1%	20.4%	45.5%	
	Team mbr 1: College degree	29.2%	23.4%	47.4%	
	Team mbr 1: Post college	36.8%	29.4%	33.8%	0.001
TM1_WKEXP	Team mbr 1: Yrs work experience (Avg)	13.01	16.14	13.91	0.000

Table 7.1: (*Continued*)

		New Firm	Active	Quit	StatSign
TM1_OTHSUS	Team mbr 1: Other start-ups (Avg)	1.03	1.03	0.81	0.144
TM_SIZEH	Start-up team size:humans only (Avg)	1.44	1.37	1.38	0.159
GR_PREF	Easy to manage	33.8%	23.5%	42.8%	
	Maxamize growth	33.3%	17.8%	48.9%	0.013
HITECH_IX	Hi tech emphasis, 0 to 3 points (Avg, max 3)	0.87	0.94	0.80	0.037
ECON_SECTOR	Extractive sectors	27.0%	38.1%	34.9%	
	Transformation sectors	34.6%	19.9%	45.5%	
	Business service sectors	33.5%	23.8%	42.7%	
	Consumer oriented sectors	34.0%	20.0%	46.0%	0.029
ACTS_SUM	Total activity initiated (Avg; max = 18)	11.3	8.00	8.30	0.000
HIRE_AW	Employee Hire	59.6%	12.1%	28.3%	0.000
GETFNDAW	Received formal funding	52.2%	14.5%	33.3%	0.000
EIN_AW	Business registration number	48.8%	19.5%	31.8%	0.000
FTWK_AW1	Devoted full time to SU	48.3%	18.1%	33.6%	0.000
SALES_AW	Initial Sales, Income	47.1%	19.8%	33.1%	0.000
SUPCRDAW	Supplier Credit	46.4%	16.5%	37.1%	0.000
SUTEAMAW	Formed start-up team	45.4%	17.0%	37.6%	0.115
LEASE_AW	Purchased, leased capital assets	41.7%	20.9%	37.4%	0.000

Table 7.1: (*Continued*)

		New Firm	Active	Quit	StatSign
PATENTAW	Patent, copyright, trademark	41.7%	18.5%	39.7%	0.000
ASKFNDAW	Asked Institution for Funds	41.2%	14.4%	44.4%	0.000
PLHLSTAW	Dedicated Phone Line, Listing	40.9%	19.7%	39.5%	0.000
FINPRJAW	Financial Projections	40.7%	16.9%	42.7%	0.000
PROMOTAW	Promoted product, services	39.7%	18.4%	41.9%	0.004
PURCHAAW	Materials, supplies, inventory	38.3%	20.8%	40.9%	0.000
ONINVAW1	Owner invested own money	35.5%	20.8%	43.8%	0.000
DFNMKTAW	Defined Markets, Customers	35.4%	19.8%	44.9%	0.000
BUSPLNAW	Business plan	35.2%	19.4%	45.4%	0.000
MODEL_AW	Model, prototype developed	34.7%	21.8%	43.5%	0.000
THINK_AW	Serious Thought	34.9%	22.0%	43.0%	0.475

Table 7.2: Independent Variables and Time to Outcome.

		Initial Profits	StatSign	Quit	StatSign	Start-up Active	StatSign
	Time from entry (avg, mths)	26.4		29.8		58.6	
COUNTRY	Australia	26.8		22.1		39.2	
	China	18.7		18.2		Miss	
	Sweden	19.2		28.7		Miss	
	United States	32.7	0.000	33.4	0.000	62.0	
TM1_SEX	Male	27.7		30.8		58.0	
	Female	24.6	0.080	28.5	0.095	59.6	0.546
TM1_AGE_6C	Team mbr 1: 18-24 yrs old	22.0		26.1		51.1	
	Team mbr 1: 25-34 yrs old	24.5		29.5		53.5	
	Team mbr 1: 35-44 yrs old	27.0		31.2		59.8	
	Team mbr 1: 45-54 yrs old	28.7		30.6		59.2	
	Team mbr 1: 55-64 yrs old	31.8		29.3		72.2	
	Team mbr 1: 65-up yrs old	18.9	0.071	27.7	0.343	64.0	0.002
TM1_EDUC	Team mbr 1: Up to high school	21.9		26.8		57.3	
	Team mbr 1: Post HS, pre coll	27.3		32.9		57.4	
	Team mbr 1: College degree	26.7		29.1		60.1	
	Team mbr 1: Post college	31.7	0.020	29.1	0.014	61.2	0.003
TM1_WKEXP	Yrs work experience (Corr)	0.12	0.002	0.15	0.000	0.18	0.568
TM1_OTHSUS	Other start-ups (Corr)	-0.03	0.498	-0.02	0.604	0.03	0.407
TM_SIZEH	Start-up team size:humans only (Corr)	0.02	0.659	-0.01	0.660	-.01	0.572
GR_PREF	Easy to manage	25.7		29.8		59.3	
	Maximize growth	27.9	0.274	29.6	0.907	55.2	0.208
HITECH_IX	Hi tech emphasis, 0 to 3 points (corr)	0.15	0.000	-0.02	0.510	-.05	0.220

Table 7.2: (*Continued*)

		Initial Profits	StatSign	Quit	StatSign	Start-up Active	StatSign
ECON_SECTOR	Extractive sectors	40.9		36.2		60.3	
	Transformation sectors	28.1		31.3		62.6	
	Business service sectors	27.8		30.8		61.8	
	Consumer oriented sectors	24.1	0.018	28.8	0.005	56.2	0.009
ACTS_SUM	Total activity initiated (Corr)	−0.40	0.000	0.02	0.472	−.12	0.006
GETFNDAW	Received formal funding	20.2	0.000	33.5	0.071	55.2	0.372
HIRE___AW	Employee Hire	20.8	0.000	29.7	0.952	57.5	0.699
FINPRJAW	Financial Projections	21.5	0.000	28.3	0.009	58.8	0.235
SUPCRDAW	Supplier Credit	22.3	0.000	29.0	0.365	58.1	0.755
PLHLSTAW	Dedicated Phone Line, Listing	22.3	0.000	30.4	0.411	58.3	0.833
PATENTAW	Patent, copyright, trademark	22.4	0.029	28.3	0.395	58.6	0.665
EIN___AW	Business registration number	23.0	0.000	34.2	0.000	62.2	0.033
FTWK_AW1	Devoted full time to SU	23.2	0.000	28.6	0.237	61.3	0.150
SALES_AW	Initial Sales, Income	23.2	0.000	33.5	0.000	60.7	0.043
BUSPLNAW	Business plan	23.7	0.000	29.0	0.025	58.6	0.000
SUTEAMAW	Formed start-up team	23.8	0.024	29.2	0.648	49.1	0.000
LEASE_AW	Purchased, leased capital assets	24.2	0.000	30.2	0.546	58.6	0.462
PROMOTAW	Promoted product, services	24.2	0.000	29.5	0.515	58.6	0.021
ONINVAW1	Owner invested own money	24.5	0.000	29.2	0.069	58.6	0.000
PURCHAAW	Materials, supplies, inventory	24.9	0.000	30.3	0.353	57.6	0.171
DFNMKTAW	Defined Markets, Customers	25.2	0.000	29.2	0.100	69.3	0.000
ASKFNDAW	Asked Institution for Funds	25.3	0.363	31.1	0.269	57.4	0.620
THINK_AW	Serious Thought	25.7	0.001	30.3	0.056	57.4	0.000
MODEL_AW	Model, prototype developed	27.2	0.110	30.7	0.033	58.6	0.699

is reported by virtually all nascent entrepreneurs by 24 months. Only efforts to form a start-up team are not related to the outcomes.

All other variables have a statistically significant association with the outcomes, including the county in which the start-up occurs, age and education and work experience of team member one, a preference for a growth firm, technological sophistication and economic sector of the new venture, and initiation of 17 different start-up activities in the first 24 months.

Identifying factors associated with the time required to reach an outcome (initial profits or disengagement), as presented in Table 7.2, reflect a more mixed result. Many factors have a statistically significant relationship to time to initial profits, with the host country, team member one educational attainment and work experience, emphasis on high technology, the economic sector of activity, amount of start-up activity in the first 24 months, as well initiating 17 of 19 activities associated with the time required to reach initial profits.

As shown in Table 7.2 the host country, educational attainment and work experience of team member one (the respondent), and 3 of 19 start-up activities have a statistically significant relationship to the time required to disengage from the activity. This would suggest that some external factors—like the development of more attractive work opportunities—may be affecting the decision to disengage.

Time active in the start-up process is presented in the two right columns of Table 7.2. The average time is 58.6 months, twice that of those achieving profits, 26.4 months, or that quit, 29.8 months. It would appear that older nascent entrepreneurs, those with more education, not in consumer oriented sectors, engaged in less start-up activities spend more time in the process. Both the total number of activities and seven specific activities are associated with more time in the start-up process.

7.1 Start-up Activity Indices

Start-up activities are not independent, unrelated efforts to implement a new firm. The inter-correlation among the activities initiated in the first 24 months is presented in Appendix B. Among the 171 correlations for the 2,015 cases, 146 are statistically significant. A factor analysis of the 18 activities, omitting serious thought about the start-up, indicated that 17 activities could be incorporated into six indices.[2]

The allocation of items to each index is provided in Table 7.3. They can be described as follows.

- **Public presence**: Any activity that indicates a public presence of the ventures, such as sales, public or administrative registry, or promotion of goods or services.

- **Operations:** Activity that involves operational activity to produce the good or service, such as full time work provided by owners, employees, or supplier relationships.

- **Infrastructure:** Activities that involve creating a physical presence, such as acquiring capital assets, supplies or inventory, or investments by the owners.

- **Planning:** Initiating of formal planning, such as financial projections, defining markets, or preparation of a business plan.

- **Funding:** Activities related to external funding, such as requests for or acquiring external financial support.

- **Complexity:** Activities associated with more complex initiatives, including the formation of a start-up team and applying for intellectual property rights.

Indices for each dimension were created by adding the number of activities reported in the first 24 months in the start-up process. This value could vary from zero (0) to two, three, or four, depending on the

---

[2]A similar exercise completed with the US PSED I cohort involved 23 start-up activities, excluding serious thought and four that involved administrative and tax registration requirements (Reynolds, 2007). The final result from a factor analysis of 648 nascent ventures was six slightly different dimensions, business presence (5 items); production implementation (6 items); organizational and financial structure (4 items); personal planning (3 items); personal preparation (3 items); and a task or product focus (2 items)

Table 7.3: Start-up Activity Indices Items.

PUBLIC PRESENCE	(0.56)*
Sales or income	Has the new business received any money, income, or fees from the sale of goods or services?
Public listing	Does the new business have its own phone or website listing? [The website option was added after the year 2000.]
Promote products or services	Have marketing or promotional efforts been started for the products or services this start-up will be selling?
Business registration	Has this new business be registered with the appropriate government agency?
OPERATIONS	(0.49)
Hired employees	Have any employees or managers been hired for pay—workers that would not share ownership?
Supplier credit	Has credit with a supplier been established?
Full-time work on the start-up	Have you (the respondent or team member one) begun to devote full time to the business—35 or more hours per week?
INFRASTRUCTURE	(0.50)
Leased, acquired major assets	Have any major items equipment, facilities or property been purchased, leased, or rented for the new start-up?
Purchased materials, parts, supplies	Have any raw materials, inventory, supplies or components been purchased/
Invested own money	Have you invested any of your own money in this business?

Table 7.3: (*Continued*)

PLANNING	(0.49)
Began business plan	Has a business plan been prepared for this start-up?
Financial projections developed	Have projected financial statements, such as income and cash flow statements, been developed?
Define markets	Has an effort been made to define the market opportunities by talking with potential customers or getting information about the competition?
FUNDING	(0.67)
Asked for funds	Have financial institutions or other people been asked for funds?
Received funds	Have you received the first outside finding from financial institutions or other people for this new business?
COMPLEXITY	(0.24)
Organized start-up team	Has a start-up team been organized?
Patent, copy, trademark filing	Has an application for a patent, copyright, or trademark relevant to this new business been submitted?
Not included	
Develop model, prototype	Has there been work on developing a model or prototype for delivery of the product or service?

*Chronhbach's Alpha measure of reliability based on first 24 months after entry.

number of items in the index. The eighteenth activity, development of a model or prototype, was not associated with any factor and its inclusion in any index lowered the reliability. As only one item is related to the implementation of a model or prototype to deliver a product, it has a value of 0 or 1. The reliability, as indicated by Chronbach's Alpha, is 0.5 or higher for five indices and 0.24 for the measure of complexity. Higher reliability would be preferred, but with a small number of dichotomous items this is the best that could be achieved. The indices are, however, easier to manage conceptually than 18 individual activities.

The association between the average value of these measures and the outcomes at 72 months is presented in Table 7.4. The entries represent the average values of the indices for each outcome. The first six rows are the multi-item indices and in every case the average value is highest for those in profit, next highest for those that have quit, and lowest for those still active in the start-up process. All differences are statistically significant. The proportion that report working on a model or prototype is highest for those in profit at 72 months, but the difference is not statistically significant.

Table 7.4: Start-up Activity Indices and Outcomes: Mean Values.

Activity Status at 24 months	Outcome status at 72 months			Stat sign.
	In Profit	Quit	Active start-up	
Public Presence	2.65	1.76	1.72	0.000
Operations	1.50	0.81	0.70	0.000
Infrastructure	2.37	1.96	1.91	0.000
Planning	2.24	2.07	1.64	0.000
Funding	0.46	0.32	0.20	0.000
Complexity	0.50	0.34	0.28	0.000
Model/Prototype	75.6%	71.4%	71.6%	0.138

The correlation between the index values and the time required to reach an outcome status or remain active in the start-up process

Table 7.5: Correlations: Start-up Activity Indices and Time to Outcomes: Correlations.

24 Month Activity Status	Outcome status at 72 months		
	In Profit	Quit	Active start-up
Public Presence	−.42	0.06	−.14
Operations	−.36	−.08	ns
Infrastructure	−.35	−.06	−.28
Planning	−.37	−.15	−.35
Funding	−.13	ns	ns
Complexity	−.14	ns	ns
Model/Prototype	ns	ns	ns

Note: ns = not statistically significant with 2-tail test at 0.05 level.

is presented in Table 7.5. Thirteen of 21 correlations are statistically significant; the other eight are not included in the table. Twelve of the correlations are negative, indicating that implementing the activity has shortened the time to reach an outcome or remain active in the start-up process. The one exception is the public presence of the nascent venture, which seems to lengthen the time before a quit occurs.

All six activity dimensions, reflecting those initiated in the first 24 months after entry into venture creation, have a statistically significant relationship with the outcomes 72 months after entry into the process; they also are related to the time required to reach one or more outcomes. There is no statistically significant relationship associated with beginning to develop a model or prototype to outcomes or the time required to reach the outcome.

8

Multi-Variate analysis: Identifying Critical Factors

It is clear that a large number of factors and activities have a statistically significant association with the outcome of participating in the start-up process. It is, however, very likely that many of these factors are interrelated—or inter-correlated; they occur together. It is of considerable interest to determine which are the most significant in determining the outcomes of the start-up process. Two strategies are pursued to facilitate this objective. The use of step-wise regression analysis to develop linear additive models incorporating the most successful factors is presented first. This is followed by a CHAID or decision tree analysis that identifies combinations of factors that are associated with different outcomes.

8.1   Linear Additive Models and Step-wise Regression

This regression assessment procedure is designed to facilitate identifying those factors that have an independent impact on a dependent variable. The dependent variables were whether or not a given case was considered in profit, discontinued, or still active 72 months after entering the start-up process. Each outcome was compared against the other two options. For example, those cases in profit were compared to those cases that had quit or were still active after 72 months. For all three assessments, a total of 2,051 cases were available for analysis. A second assessment focused on the time in the start-up process before an outcome occurred. In this case, only those reporting each type of outcome after 72 months could be included in the assessment. As a result, 705 cases were included in the assessment of time to reach profits, 877 for the time to quit, and 266 for the time remaining active in the start-up process.

The independent variables were restricted to those that occurred or were measured in the first 24 months after entry into the start-up process. This was straightforward for many features determined at the start of the process, such as the gender or age of the key respondent or the size of the start-up team. For the start-up activities this involved tracking those initiated in the first 24 months, concurrent with the identification of the outcome variables (Table 5.1) for about one-third of the cases. For these cases the assessment is cross-sectional. A majority, however, had not reported outcomes in the first 24 months so for these cases the assessment is related to outcomes in the future.

The results are presented in Table 8.1.[1] The standardized beta values are presented for all independent variables included as making a statistically significant independent contribution in a linear additive model predicting the six dependent variables. Both the factors included and not included in these models are of some interest.

The success of these models is mixed. The explained variance of the models predicting outcomes varies from 10 to 20%. This probably reflects two factors. First, the use of binary or dichotomous dependent variables reduces the potential for accurate predictions with linear additive models. Second, it is very likely that other factors or processes, not represented among the independent variables, also affect these outcomes. Nonetheless, these models do suggest that some statistically significant factors have been identified.

---

[1]The regression analysis utilized the SPSS V 23 REGRESSION module with the standard defaults for all modeling criteria.

Table 8.1: Linear Additive Models: Outcomes and Time to Outcomes.

		72 MONTH OUTCOME			TIME TO OUTCOME		
		Profit	Quit	Active	Profit	Quit	Active
	Number of cases	2,051	2,051	2,051	705	877	266
	Explained variance	20.4%	11.3%	10.3%	27.7%	9.0%	46.8%
	Constant	−8.71	70.92	38.07	43.80	28.91	116.26
CTRY_AU	Australia = 1	0.07	−0.20	0.14		−0.20	−0.56
CTRY_CH	China = 1	0.18	−0.12	−0.07	−0.22	−0.23	
CTRY_SE	Sweden = 1	0.13	−0.15		−0.21	−0.14	
CTRY_US	United States = 1	Base	Base	Base	Base	Base	Base
TM1_SEX	Gender: Female = 0, Male = 1						
TM1_1824	Team mbr 1: 18-24 yrs old =1	Base	Base	Base	Base	Base	Base
TM1_2534	Team mbr 1: 25-34 yrs old =1						
TM1_3544	Team mbr 1: 35-44 yrs old =1						
TM1_4554	Team mbr 1: 45-54 yrs old =1						
TM1_5564	Team mbr 1: 55-64 yrs old =1						0.12
TM1_6598	Team mbr 1: 65-up yrs old =1						
TM1_ED0012	Team mbr 1: Up to high school	Base	Base	Base	Base	Base	Base
TM1_ED1315	Team mbr 1: Post HS, pre coll					0.08	
TM1_ED1616	Team mbr 1: College degree	−0.07		0.07			

(Continued)

Table 8.1: (*Continued*)

		72 MONTH OUTCOME			TIME TO OUTCOME		
		Profit	Quit	Active	Profit	Quit	Active
TM1_ED1720	Team mbr 1: Post college		−0.10	0.08			
TM1_OTHSUS	Team mbr 1: Start-up start-up experience						
TM!_WKEXP	Team mbr 1: Work experience		−0.08	0.10			
TM_SIZEH	Team size: Total owners, human						
GR_PREF	Easy manage = 0, growth = 1	−0.05	0.05		0.10		
HITECH_IX	Hi tech emphasis, 0 to 3 points				0.08		
SEC_EXTR	Extractive sectors = 1	Base	Base	Base	Base	Base	Base
SEC_TRANS	Transformation sectors = 1						
SEC_BUSSER	Business service sectors = 1						
SEC_CONSER	Consumer oriented sectors = 1						
ACTS_SUM024	Total activity initiated (max = 18)	0.30	−0.17	−0.16			
PROMOT_024	Promotion index: 4 items	0.13	−0.10		−0.28		
INFRST_024	Infrastructure index: 3 items				−0.14		−0.28
OPERAT_024	Operational index: 3 items	0.09	−0.09		−0.13		
FUNDIN_024	Funding index: 2 items						
PLANIN_024	Future planning index: 3 items	−0.12	0.22	−0.11			−0.21
INNOVA_024	Innovation index: 2 items						

The two major groups of factors associated with predictions of the outcome are the national context and start-up activities. It is quite clear that the United States provides a unique context, for in Australia, China, and Sweden more cases report initial profits, fewer report quitting, and times to reach outcomes are generally equal to or shorter than cases in the United States.

In terms of start-up activity, more activity in the first 24 months has a significant impact on achieving profits and less activity is related to more quits or more cases still active after 72 months.

Four of the six start-up activity domains have a statistically significant contribution to predicting one or more of the six dependent variables. An emphasis on promotion or developing an operational business is associated with achieving profitability and less disengagement; they are also associated with achieving profitability sooner. Work on creating an infrastructure is associated with a reduced time to profit and less time active in the start-up process.

The impact of explicit planning is mixed, for is associated with fewer nascents in profit, more that discontinue or quit, and fewer that are still active in the process.[2] It is also associated with a less time active in the start-up process.

There is no independent contribution of attention given to external funding or innovation activities, forming a team or pursuing intellectual property rights. While these may be critical for many ventures, they apparently occur in conjunction with other activities.

Compared to the national context and start-up activities, background of the entrepreneur and the nature of the venture seem to have less influence. For example, there is NO gender effect. Gender is not related to either different outcomes or the time involved in reaching these outcomes.

Age of the respondent is included in only one model that related to time active in the process. Compared to those 18-54 years old those 55 to 64 years old are in the start-up for a longer period of time. But age is not related to whether the venture achieves profits or discontinues or the time required to achieve these outcomes.

---

[2]In the model tracking the effects of activity in the first 36 months in the start-up process (not shown), future planning leads to quicker profitability.

The effect of educational attainment is also modest. Compared to those that have no gone beyond high school those with college degrees are less likely to achieve profits, those with graduate experience are less likely to quit, and those with either college degrees or graduate experience are more likely to still be active in a start-up after 72 months.

More work experience seems to reduce the tendency to quit, but increase the tendency to stay active in the start-up process. Those planning for a growth firm are less likely to reach profits and more likely to quit. A venture with a technological emphasis is likely to take longer to reach initial profitability.

Finally, there is no impact associated with the economic sector in which the new venture will operate.

8.2   Identifying Interaction among Start-up Factors

The step-wise regression procedure is useful in developing a linear additive model of factors affecting the outcomes of the firm creation process. It identifies the factors that are assumed to have an independent effect on the outcomes. The final model is the sum of the individual effects of a variety of features, assumed to be unrelated. While the additive effect of several actions clearly has an impact on whether a nascent venture reaches initial profits or is abandoned, identifying the joint impact of several activities presents a different challenge. Information about the joint impact of two or more factors, such as the tendency of more experienced start-up teams to engage in business planning, can be done with trial and error specifications for regression analysis or the use of other analysis procedures.

A procedure to identify important interactions among independent variables has been developed. Various referred to as a CHAID (Chi Square Automatic Interaction Detection) or TREE (for creating a decision tree structure) analysis it involves a sequence of assessments. A number of factors that may affect a dependent variable are identified. The procedure identifies the most important factor affecting a dependent variable, such as reports of initial profits 72 months after entry into the start-up process. The sample is then divided into subsamples based on the impact of the single most significant factor. For example, gender of the informant may be related to different outcomes. If so, the sample is divided into two sub-samples, one including all cases involved men and the other all cases involving women. The next stage is to consider which of the remaining factors has a major impact on each sub-sample, and different factors may be selected for each subsample. A number of second stage subgroups are then identified. The procedure continues with each subsample until there are no statistically significant differences provided by the remaining independent variables, the number of cases in a subset becomes too small for further assessment, or the number of levels of analysis becomes difficult to interpret. The following assessments are based on three rounds of assessment providing a three level decision tree.[3]

The result of the assessment using factors identified and acts initiated in the first 24 months on achieving profitability after 72 months is presented in Table 8.2; 18 distinct subgroups are defined. The first column provides the features identified in the first three rounds of assessment that provides a description of each group, separated by a double forward slash. The second column indicates the percentage of the total sample in each group. The third column provides the proportion of those that reported initial profits in each group. The three right columns indicates the proportion of each group reporting profits, still active in the start-up, or disengaged after 72 months. Each group is identified with a letter at the beginning of each row.

The proportion that are profitable ranges from 86.2% of those in row A to 4.7% of those in row R, the high/low ratio is about 18. This is, to be noted, much greater variation in the dependent variable than the 20% of variance accounted for by the linear additive model provided in Table 8.2. There is also a substantial range of differences among

---

[3]The TREE procedure in SPSS V 23 was utilized with appropriate weights. The procedure rounds all weights to an integer value, so cases with weights less than 0.5 were reset for the analysis to 0.50, which were rounded up to a value of 1. The proportion with outcomes and the time lag with outcomes were computed after cases were assigned to decision tree groups using the case weights adjusted for start-up team size. As a result, the number of cases varies somewhat for the different assessments.

Table 8.2: Interaction Models: Predicting Outcomes.

Group Characteristics	% Total Sample	% Those in Profit	72 Month Outcome		
			% Group in profit	% Group start-up active	% Group quits
A: 12-18 SU Acts//AU,CH,SE//0,1 other start-up experiences	7.1%	18.7%	86.2%	5.6%	8.2%
B: 12-18 SU Acts//AU,CH,SE//2+ other start-up experiences	1.6%	3.2%	65.8%	13.2%	18.9%
C: 9-11 SU Acts//AU,CH,SE//High promotions (3,4)	7.0%	12.3%	58.9%	14.9%	26.2%
D: 12-18 SU Acts//U.S.//Not growth oriented	8.2%	14.3%	56.6%	16.2%	27.1%
E: 6-8 SU Acts//Low planning (0,1)//0-1 yr work experience	1.5%	2.3%	53.3%	10.0%	36.7%
F: 12-18 SU Acts//U.S.//Growth oriented	3.3%	4.0%	36.4%	6.1%	56.7%
G: 6-8 SU Acts//Low planning (0,1)//6-20 yrs work experience	5.9%	6.8%	38.8%	16.4%	44.4%
H: 9-11 SU Acts//AU,CH,SE//Low promotions (0,1,2)	5.9%	6.5%	40.2%	22.7%	37.1%
I: 6-8 SU Acts//Higher planning (2,3)//Grad educ	2.7%	2.7%	29.6%	24.1%	46.3%
J: 9-11 SU Acts//U.S.//Some operational (1,2,3)	12.4%	10.6%	28.3%	19.7%	52.2%
K: 2-5 SU Acts//Buss services//	4.4%	3.6%	23.9%	38.5%	38.0%
L: 2-5 SU Acts//Extrac, Transform, Cons Serv//Grad educ	1.9%	1.1%	18.9%	41.7%	37.8%
M: 2-5 SU Acts//Extrac, Transform, Cons Serv//Up to HS Degree	14.9%	6.8%	16.4%	28.8%	54.5%
N: 2-5 SU Acts//Higher planning (2,3)//Up to Coll Degree	5.4%	2.4%	14.6%	23.3%	62.1%
O: 6-8 SU Acts//Low planning (0,1)//2-5 yrs work experience	1.4%	0.6%	13.8%	41.4%	44.8%
P: 9-11 SU Acts//U.S.//No operational (0)	4.4%	1.7%	11.1%	13.5%	74.4%
Q: 6-8 SU Acts//Low planning (0,1)//Over 20 yrs work experience	3.1%	0.9%	9.7%	35.5%	54.8%
R: 2-5 SU Acts//Extrac, Transform, Cons Serv//Post HS, Coll degree	8.8%	1.4%	4.7%	42.4%	52.9%

those that quit, with 8% in row A to 74% in row P, which is nine times higher. Variations in those that remain in the start-up process ranges from 5.6% for those in row A to 42.4% of those in row R; seven times higher. Nascent ventures in these different groups are associated with wide differences in the outcomes.

Perhaps most striking is the diversity in the patterns of outcomes for the different sets of factors. The top two rows, A and B, represent those that initiated 12 or more activities located in Australia, China, and Sweden and two-thirds or more report initial profits. These two groups are about 9% of the sample. The single largest group, row M, are 15% of the sample associated with 5 or fewer acts related to a nascent venture in extractive, transformation, or business service sectors initiated by a person with up to a high school degree, 16% have achieved initial profits and 54% have quit. The largest proportion of those that achieve initial profits (14.3%) are row D, ventures associated with 12 or more start-up activities in the United States that are not growth oriented; 56.6% manage to reach initial profits.

The outcomes are presented graphically for each group in Figure 8.1. Moving from the top to the bottom of the figure makes clear that there are fewer that reach profits and more quits associated with the groups at the bottom. The proportion still active after 72 months is low at 6% at for very top and is somewhat larger as one move down the figure. But both the proportion that remains active and disengages varies somewhat among the groups defined by the proportion that become profitable. This suggests that other processes would be involved in affecting the disposition of those that do not achieve initial profits.

One striking feature of this assessment is the absence of specific start-up activities. In 18 groups specific start-up activities are included in 6 cases in the second round and four cases in the third round of assessment. This lack of inclusion probably reflects the high correlation of any specific activity with the overall level of start-up activity, which is identified as the single most important factor affecting the potential for profitability. An assessment to adjust for this factor is discussed below.

The relationships between the proportion that reach different outcomes and the time to reach the outcome if presented in Table 8.3. The

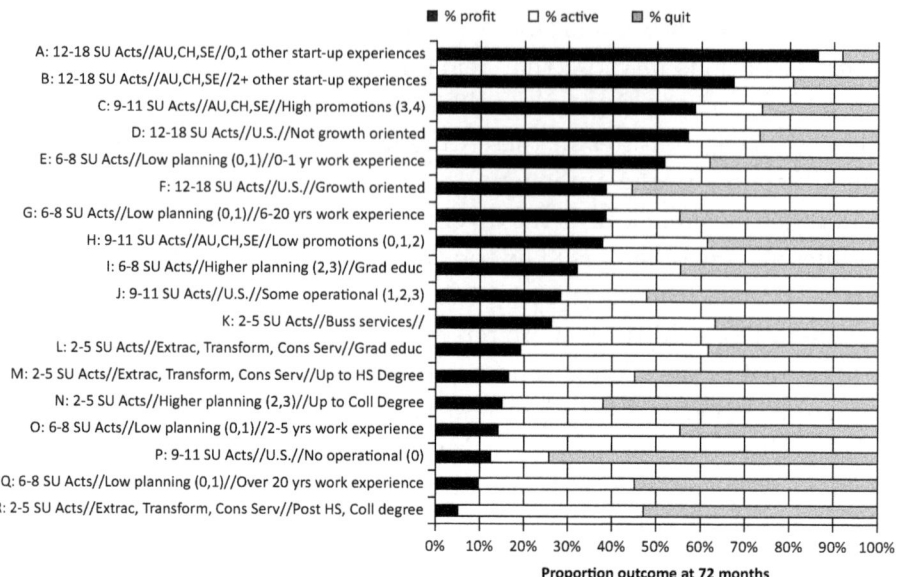

Figure 8.1: Interaction Model Groups and Outcomes.

correlation among the different groups for each outcome is provided in the bottom row.

The time to reach profits varies from 14 months for Row A to 72 months (6 years) for groups represented by rows L and R, a range of 58 months. There is a strong negative relationship between these two outcomes, negative correlation across 18 groups of minus 0.77. The higher the proportion that reaches profits, the shorter the time required.

The same comparison is provided for those that quit. The time required to quit ranges from 21 to 22 months (see rows A, H, I) to 36 months (rows K and R); a range of 15 months. In this case, there is a positive correlation (0.45); those groups with the highest proportion of quits are associated with a longer time to quit. The underlying processes associated with disengagement appear to be quite different from those associated with achieving initial profits.

The relationship between the proportion still active and the time they have been active in the start-up process is presented in the two right columns of Table 8.3. Time in the start-up process varies from

Table 8.3: Interaction Models: Outcomes and Time to Outcomes.

Group Characteristics	In Profit	Time to profit (Mths)	Quit	Time to quit (Mths)	Still active	Time still active (Mths)
A: 12-18 SU Acts//AU,CH,SE//0,1 other start-up experiences	86.6%	14.2	8.2%	22.6	5.6%	26.3
B: 12-18 SU Acts//AU,CH,SE//2+ other start-up experiences	65.8%	16.1	18.9%	22.9	13.2%	32.6
C: 9-11 SU Acts//AU,CH,SE//High promotions (3,4)	57.9%	15.5	26.2%	23.3	14.9%	69.8
D: 12-18 SU Acts//U.S.//Not growth oriented	57.7%	19.0	27.1%	34.8	16.2%	53.3
E: 6-8 SU Acts//Low planning (0,1)//0-1 yr work experience	50.0%	28.5	36.7%	23.8	10.0%	92.5
F: 12-18 SU Acts//U.S.//Growth oriented	39.4%	23.9	56.7%	33.8	6.1%	78.0
G: 6-8 SU Acts//Low planning (0,1)//6-20 yrs work experience	38.1%	30.3	44.4%	26.9	16.4%	27.8
H: 9-11 SU Acts//AU,CH,SE//Low promotions (0,1,2)	36.4%	18.3	37.1%	21.2	22.7%	74.6
I: 6-8 SU Acts//Higher planning (2,3)//Grad educ	33.3%	34.1	46.3%	22.2	24.1%	83.3
J: 9-11 SU Acts//U.S.//Some operational (1,2,3)	28.3%	32.8	52.2%	30.9	19.7%	95.8
K: 2-5 SU Acts//Buss services//	27.3%	51.2	38.0%	36.3	38.5%	103.0
L: 2-5 SU Acts//Extrac, Transform, Cons Serv//Grad educ	18.9%	72.1	37.8%	33.6	41.7%	90.2
M: 2-5 SU Acts//Extrac, Transform, Cons Serv//Up to HS Degree	16.4%	36.5	54.5%	30.3	28.8%	64.4
N: 2-5 SU Acts//Higher planning (2,3)//Up to Coll Degree	15.2%	36.6	62.1%	27.3	23.3%	53.6
O: 6-8 SU Acts//Low planning (0,1)//2-5 yrs work experience	14.3%	38.8	44.8%	24.5	41.4%	76.6
P: 9-11 SU Acts//U.S.//No operational (0)	12.5%	36.8	74.4%	33.2	13.5%	76.5
Q: 6-8 SU Acts//Low planning (0,1)//Over 20 yrs work experience	9.8%	57.3	54.8%	31.2	35.5%	90.4
R: 2-5 SU Acts//Extrac, Transform, Cons Serv//Post HS, Coll degree	5.1%	71.9	52.9%	35.7	42.4%	
Correlation: Outcome proportion and time to outcome	−0.77		0.45		0.43	

26 months (Row A) to 103 months (Row l); a range of 77 months or over six years. As with those ventures that quit, the relationship across the groups is positive, a correlation of 0.43. Those nascent ventures in groups where the proportion still active is the highest have been in the start-up process for the longest period of time.

While there are clear patterns associated with the three outcomes, there are also some interesting unique situations. The group in row A of Table 8.2 and Figure 8.1 are 7% of the total sample but 19% of those that achieved profits; 86% of this group did this in 14 months. They initiated 12 or more activities, were located in Australia, China, and Sweden and had limited experience with start-ups. It would be interesting to know more about how they moved forward with their venture.

At the other extreme is the group represented by row R of Table 8.2 and Figure 8.1. They are 9% of the sample but where one in 20, 4.7%, achieved initial profits, taking 72 months—6 years—to do so. They engaged in less than 6 start-up activities in the first two years, were emphasizing a venture in the extractive, transformation, or consumer services sectors, and the principal had gone beyond high school or completed college. While slightly more than half had given up, 42% were still actively trying to implement this venture after 72 months, having been involved an average of 90 months.

An intermediate example would be those nascent ventures represented by Row F in Table 8.2. While 36% achieved initial profits in two years, 57% had quit in 33 months, leaving only 6% still active in the process for 92 months—almost 8 years. This is a very active group that initiated 12 or more activities in the first 24 months, are all located in the U.S. and are growth oriented. Those associated with most of the ventures, 57%, appear to have tested the potential of the venture and decided the growth was inadequate. It would be interesting to know more about how this decision was developed.

Overall, the decision tree analysis helps to locate groups of nascents with very different outcomes. The three characteristics that define each group provide an initial, but incomplete, description of their situation and activity.

8.3 Overview: Factors Affecting Outcomes and Times to Outcomes

Two different assessments of the effect of factors identified in the first 24 months of the start-up process on the 72 month outcomes were completed.[4] The results are summarized in Table 8.4, with significant factors in the step-wise regression models identified by nature of the impact in the left column for each outcome and the level in the decision tree hierarchy reported in the right column.

Several features of the start-up period dominate the summary. Total start-up activity completed in the first 24 months, the national context, and the emphasis on planning activity has an impact in all analyses. The only personal characteristic to be included in all assessments is educational attainment.

Both an emphasis on promotion and operational start-up activities and a growth orientation are included in the assessments related to achieving initial profits or quitting. Other factors are found in different assessments, with varying levels of impact.

The nature of the impact of the most significant factors is not always as might be expected.

- More start-up activity is consistently associated with more firms in profit, less that quit, and less continuing active in the start-up process.

- Compared to nascent ventures in the U.S., those in Australia, China, and Sweden are more likely to achieve profits, less likely to quit and less likely to continue in the start-up process.

- Business planning is associated with a reduced tendency to achieve initial profits or remain in the start-up process and an increased tendency to quit.

- In general, pursuing other start-up activities such as promoting

---

[4]Three level decision trees were completed with quits and still active at 72 months as the dependent variables; this summary reflects these analyses in addition to the decision tree for initial profits.

Table 8.4: Factors with Impacts on Outcomes: Overview.[5]

	Initial profits		Quit		Still active	
	Reg	Tree	Reg	Tree	Reg	Tree
Country (Not U.S.)	++	**	++	**/*	++/-	**/*
Number of SU Acts	+++	***	–	***	–	***
Promotion SU Activity	++	*	–			
Operation SU Activity	+	*	-			
Planning SU Activity	–	**	++	**	–	**
Innovation SU Activity						*
Funding SU Activity						*
Infrastructure SU Activity						
Develop model						
Growth orientation	-	*	+	*		
Technological emphasis				*		
Economic sector		**				
Educational attainment	-	*	–	*	+	*
Work experience		*	-		++	*
Start-up experience		*				
Age						
Gender						

Regression model standardized beta >0.19 = + + +/—; >0.10, <0.19 = ++/−; <0.10 +/−. First level tree = ***, 2$^\text{nd}$ level = **, 3$^\text{rd}$ level = *.

the new venture or developing an operating business is associated with more firms in profit and less than have quit.

- An interest in developing a growth business is associated with fewer reaching profits and more that discontinue.

- Educational attainment has mixed effects, generally those with more education are less likely to reach profits or quit and stay in the start-up process longer.

A number of other factors present in the first 24 months, such as gender, age, economic sector, experience with other start-ups, have

---

[5]Results of decision tree analysis for predicting quits and still active in the start-up provided in Appendix Tables C.1 and C.2.

Table 8.5: Factors with Impacts on Time to Outcomes: Overview.[6]

	Time to profits		Time to Quit		Time still active	
	Reg	Tree	Reg	Tree	Reg	Tree
Country (Not U.S.)	—	**/*	—	***	—	***
Number of SU Acts		***				
Promotion SU Activity	—					
Operation SU Activity	—					
Planning SU Activity				**	—	
Innovation SU Activity						
Funding SU Activity		*				
Infrastructure SU Activity	—				—	**
Growth orientation	++					
Technology emphasis	+					
Economic sector				*		
Educational attainment			+			
Work experience						
Start-up experience						
Age		**/*		*	+	
Gender		*				

Regression model standardized beta $>0.19 = +++/---$; $>0.10, <0.19 = ++/--$; $<0.10 +/-$. First level tree $=$ ***, 2nd level $=$ **, 3rd level $=$ *.

modest effects or the impact varies depending on the presence of other factors.

A similar summary of the effects on the time to reach outcomes is provided in Table 8.5. There are fewer significant factors and fewer universal patterns. This reflects the smaller sample sizes associated with focusing on those defined by their status after 72 months in the start-up process.

The only feature that is uniform across all six assessments of the time required to reach an outcome is the national context. Those start-ups in Australia, China, and Sweden appear to reach profits sooner, disengage sooner, and spend less time in the start-up process compared to

---

[6]Results of decision tree assessments related to time to reach outcomes provided in Appendix tables C.3, C.4 and C.5.

those in the U.S.[7] A growth orientation and a venture taking advantage of technological advances appear to take longer to reach profitability. More start-up activities in the first 24 months, particularly with an emphasis on promotion, operations, and infrastructure, are associated with a reduced time to initial profits. An impact of age is found only in the decision tree analysis, perhaps because it is nonlinear; mid-career adults seem to take longer to achieve outcomes than those that are young adults or senior adults. Men may take a little longer to reach profitability than women.

Following the impact of the national context, the U.S. cases take longer to quit, very few factors affect this time window. Planning, operating in the consumer services sector, and being a mid-career adult may be associated with a shorter time to disengagement.

National context is also a major factor associated with time in the start-up process, which is longest for the United States nascent ventures. An emphasis on planning and developing infrastructure seems to reduce the time in the start-up process; leading nascent entrepreneurs to either initial profits or disengagement.

---

[7]It is also possible that the U.S. data collection procedures retained a higher proportion of marginal nascent entrepreneurs who were less committed to creating new ventures.

9

Which Activities affect Start-up Outcomes

The impact of different activities, as represented by the six indices, is difficult to determine due to the major impact of the total number of start-up activities initiated in the first 24 months. The total number of activities would be highly correlated with the implementation of any activities, which would mask the impact of specific activities. It is possible that the impact of different activities will be easier to determine if the assessments were repeated without this independent variable.

9.1 Linear Additive Models and Step-wise Regression

The result of the step-wise regression that provides a linear additive model is provided in Table 9.1. The total number of start-up acts has been omitted from the list of independent variables.

All other variables are retained and the number of cases in each assessment remains the same. Omitting these variables has almost no impact on the total explained variance, suggesting that a shift to specific activities indices provides equally accurate predictive models.

Comparing the results of the two assessments (Tables 8.1 and 9.1) indicates that in all three predictions of outcomes, additional

Table 9.1: Linear Additive Models: Outcomes and Time to Outcomes (without total acts).

		72 MONTH OUTCOME			TIME TO OUTCOME		
		Profit	Quit	Active	Profit	Quit	Active
Number of cases		2,051	2,051	2,051	705	877	266
Explained variance		20.3%	11.5%	10.0%	27.7%	9.0%	46.8%
Constant		−7.75	71.88	34.06	43.81	28.91	116.26
CTRY_AU	Australia = 1, otherwise = 0	0.06	−0.20	−0.15		−0.20	−0.56
CTRY_CH	China = 1, otherwise = 0	0.16	−0.16	−0.06	−0.22	−0.23	
CTRY_SE	Sweden = 1, otherwise = 0	0.12	−0.12		−0.21	−0.14	
CTRY_US	United States = 1, otherwise = 0	Base	Base	Base	Base	Base	Base
TM1_SEX	Gender: Female = 0, Male = 1						
TM1_1824	Team mbr 1: 18-24 yrs old =1	Base	Base	Base	Base	Base	Base
TM1_2534	Team mbr 1: 25-34 yrs old =1						
TM1_3544	Team mbr 1: 35-44 yrs old =1						
TM1_4554	Team mbr 1: 45-54 yrs old =1						
TM1_5564	Team mbr 1: 55-64 yrs old =1						0.12
TM1_6598	Team mbr 1: 65-up yrs old =1						
TM1_ED0012	Team mbr 1: Up to high school	Base	Base	Base	Base	Base	Base
TM1_ED1315	Team mbr 1: Post HS, pre coll					0.08	

(Continued)

Table 9.1: (*Continued*)

		72 MONTH OUTCOME			TIME TO OUTCOME		
		Profit	Quit	Active	Profit	Quit	Active
TM1_ED1616	Team mbr 1: College degree	-.06		0.07			
TM1_ED1720	Team mbr 1: Post college		-.09	0.08			
TM1_OTHSUS	Team mbr 1: Start-up experience						
TM!_WKEXP	Team mbr 1: Work experience		-0.08	0.10			
TM_SIZEH	Team size: Total owners, human						
GR_PREF	Easy manage = 0, growth = 1	-.05	0.05		0.10		
HITECH_IX	Hi tech emphasis, 0 to 3 points-				0.08		
SEC_EXTR	Extractive sectors = 1	Base	Base	Base	Base	Base	Base
SEC_TRANS	Transformation sectors = 1						
SEC_BUSSER	Business service sectors = 1		-0.05				
SEC_CONSER	Consumer oriented sectors = 1						
PROMOT_024	Promotion index: 4 items	0.24	-0.16	-.09	-0.28		
INFRST_024	Infrastructure index: 3 items	0.08	-0.06		-0.14		-0.28
OPERAT_024	Operational index: 3 items	0.18	-0.14	-0.05	-0.13		
FUNDIN_024	Funding index: 2 items						
PLANIN_024	Future planning index: 3 items		0.17	-0.17			-0.21
INNOVA_024	Innovation index: 2 items	0.08	-0.05				

start-up activities are incorporated in the models. The model predicting profitability indicates that infrastructure and innovation activity increases the potential for profitability; the planning activity index is not included. The model predicting quits indicates that attention to infrastructure and innovation activities reduces the potential for this outcome; it also includes an indication that start-up in business services are less likely to quit. The model predicting continuation in the start-up process has a coefficient indicating that business planning is associated with a reduction of persisting in the start-up process.

There are no changes in the magnitude or direction of the coefficients in the three models related to the time associated with the three outcomes.

This new assessment provides additional information about the association of different start-up activities with the outcomes of the firm creation process.

9.2   Identifying Interaction among Start-up Activities

The results of decision tree assessments without the inclusion of the number of specific activities based on the proportion that reach initial profits are provided in Table 9.2 and Figure 9.1. Table 9.2 is organized like the previous presentation, Table 8.2, with the first column describing each of the groups, the next one indicating the proportion of the total sample in the group, the third the proportion of all those that achieve profit in the group, and the three far right indicating the proportion in the group that achieve profit, are still active in the start-up, or have quit after 72 months.

The relationships from the top to bottom of the bar chart in Figure 9.1 are relatively consistent. The proportion of quits offsets the proportions that reach profits; the proportion still active at 72 months seems to increase in the bottom part of the Figure 9.1.

As before, there is substantial variation in the proportion that achieves profit among the 19 groups. From 10% of the bottom group, row S in Table 9.2, that are profitable to 86% in the most successful group, Row A, an eight-fold difference. The diversity among groups in

Table 9.2: Interaction Models: Start-up Indices and Outcomes (without total acts).

	% Total sample	% Those in profit	% Profit	% SU Active	% Quit
A: Highest operational (3)//AU, CH, SE//25-64 Years old	4.2%	10.9%	86.0%	5.0%	9.0%
B: More operational (2)//More promotions (2,3)	4.5%	9.6%	68.6%	10.8%	21.6%
C: More operational (2)//High promotions (3)//AU, CH, SE	4.2%	8.2%	62.9%	14.6%	22.7%
D: Low operational (1)//High promotions (3,4)//AU, CH, SE	5.2%	9.4%	62.0%	13.0%	25.0%
E: More operational (2)//Some promotion (1,2)//China	1.9%	3.3%	56.4%	5.1%	38.5%
F: Highest operational (3)//United States	3.9%	6.1%	51.9%	13.0%	35.1%
G: No operational (0)//High promotions (3,4)//AU, SE, US	3.3%	5.2%	50.0%	26.6%	21.9%
H: Low operational (1)//Low promotions (0,1)//Grad Education	1.4%	2.1%	46.4%	25.0%	32.1%
I: Highest operational (3)//AU, CH, SE//18-24 Years old	1.3%	1.8%	45.8%	0.0%	54.2%
J: Low operational (1)//More promotions (2)//High infrastructure (3)	2.9%	3.6%	41.7%	23.0%	35.0%
K: More operational (2)//High promotions (3)//United States	2.9%	3.3%	35.1%	23.2%	42.9%
L: Low operational (1)//High promotions (3,4)//United States	8.5%	9.0%	33.3%	20.0%	46.5%
M: More operational (2)//Some promotion (1,2)//AU, SE, US	5.5%	5.5%	34.5%	18.2%	47.3%
N: No operational (0)//Some promotion (0,1,2)//Low planning (0,1)	12.7%	7.6%	19.7%	42.6%	37.8%
O: Low operational (1)//More promotions (2)//Some infrastructure (0,1,2)	4.1%	2.1%	19.3%	22.9%	57.8%
P: No operational (0)//High promotions (3,4)//United States	5.5%	2.9%	16.8%	20.4%	62.3%
Q: Low operational (1)//Low promotions (0,1)//Up to coll degree	8.8%	3.2%	13.2%	26.0%	60.8%
R: No operational (0)//Some promotion (0,1,2)//Some planning (2,3)	17.8%	5.8%	11.2%	23.4%	65.4%
S: More operational (2)//United States	1.4%	0.3%	10.3%	34.5%	55.2%

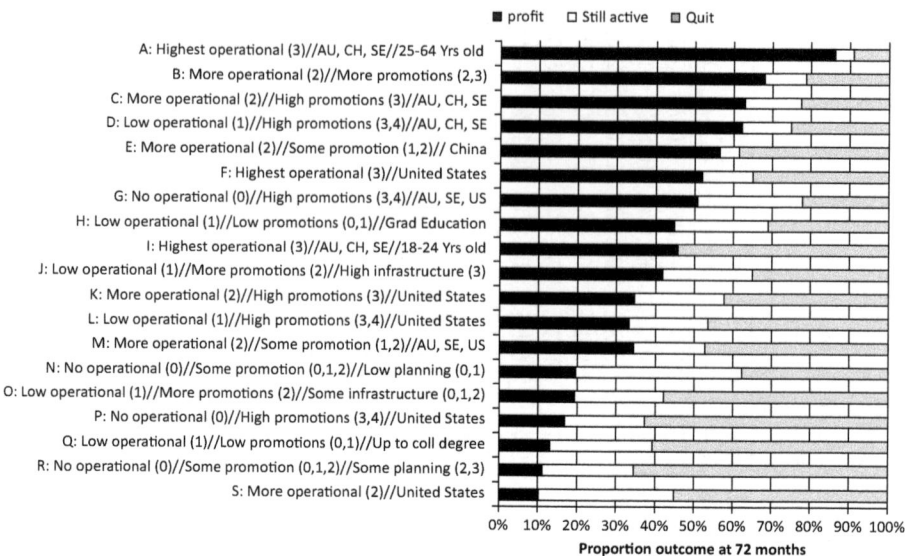

Figure 9.1: Interactive Model Groups and Outcomes (without total acts).

the proportion that are still active at 72 months varies from 0% for the row I group to 43% for the row N group. Although somewhat less, the variation in the proportion of quits is from 9% for the row A group to 65% for the row R group, which is seven times higher.

The primary emphasis in defining these groups are the start-up activities pursed in the first 24 months. The first round of assessment sorts the groups based on the emphasis on operational activities that would facilitate providing the goods or services. In the second round the initiation of promotion of the venture is associated with 16 groups; the host country is associated with three groups. In the third round assessment attention to planning and infrastructure are significant, as are national context, educational attainment, and age.

Other features of the start-up, such as technological emphasis or economic sector or growth aspirations, or the nascent entrepreneurs, such as prior experience in work or with start-ups or age or gender, are not included as related to the proportion that achieve profits.

The average time to reach profitability for each outcome is provided for the groups in Table 9.3. The average time to reach profitability varies from 10 months (Row I) to 51 months (Row N). As before, shown in Table 8.3, there is a strong negative correlation (-0.72) between the proportion that achieve profits and the time required to reach profitability. The higher the likelihood of profits, quicker this occurs.

As shown in Table 9.3, the time required to disengage varies from 14 months (Row A) to 39 months (Rows B). This is similar to that found among decision tree groups based on all initial factors. However, this is a major shift in the relationship to the time from entry to quit. Rather than a modest positive correlation, there is no relationship, the correlation is 0.06. Shifting the emphasis to start-up indices in the decision tree analysis has provided a different perspective on the relationship to the time to quit. The total number of start-up activities seems to shorten the time from entry to disengagement.

The relationship between those still active and the time in the start-up process is also presented in the two right columns of Table 9.3. With this revised assessment the range of times in the process is slightly reduced. The difference between the longest average of 93 months (Row S) and the shortest average of 38 months (Row D) is 55 months, compared to 77 months. The relationship between the proportion that are still active and the time in the process is positive, r = 0.38; this is about the same as 0.43 in the previous assessment. Groups with a higher probability of remaining active in the start-up process have a higher average length of time in the process.

The major benefit of this assessment is that it makes clear that a variety of start-up activities, particularly those related to implementing operations, promotion of the good and service and future planning are related to the outcomes. However, it would appear that the effect can vary depending on other factors—mostly not specified—that are associated with the start-up efforts. A more complete understanding of the role of start-up activities, which would improve the precision of the predictions, requires information not available at this time.

Table 9.3: Interaction Models: Outcomes and Time to Outcomes (without total acts).

Group Characteristics	In Profit	Time to profit (Mths)	Quit	Time to quit (Mths)	Still Active	Time still active (Mths)
A: Highest operational (3)//AU, CH, SE// 25-64 Years old	86.0%	15.9	9.0%	14.5	5.0%	53.6
B: More operational (2)//More promotions (2,3)	68.6%	18.1	21.6%	39.3	10.8%	72.1
C: More operational (2)//High promotions (3)//AU, CH, SE	62.9%	14.5	22.7%	23.7	14.6%	
D: Low operational (1)//High promotions (3,4)//AU, CH, SE	62.0%	18.0	25.0%	25.2	13.0%	38.3
E: More operational (2)//Some promotion (1,2)//China	56.4%	20.1	38.5%	17.5	5.1%	
F: Highest operational (3)//United States	51.9%	18.4	35.1%	32.1	13.0%	84.6
G: No operational (0)//High promotions (3,4)//AU, SE, US	50.0%	22.0	21.9%	25.1	26.6%	41.1
H: Low operational (1)//Low promotions (0,1)//Grad Education	46.4%	45.0	32.1%	31.4	25.0%	67.3
I: Highest operational (3)//AU, CH, SE//18-24 Years old	45.8%	10.5	54.2%	18.0	0.0%	
J: Low operational (1)//More promotions (2)//High infrastructure (3)	41.7%	34.1	35.0%	33.6	23.0%	61.1
K: More operational (2)//High promotions (3)//United States	35.1%	29.3	42.9%	26.7	23.2%	81.2
M: More operational (2)//Some promotion (1,2)//AU, SE, US	34.5%	25.1	47.3%	29.8	18.2%	91.6
L: Low operational (1)//High promotions (3,4)//United States	33.3%	28.2	46.5%	31.9	20.0%	83.3
N: No operational (0)//Some promotion (0,1,2)//Low planning (0,1)	19.7%	51.1	37.8%	39.1	42.6%	93.0
O: Low operational (1)//More promotions (2)//Some infrastructure (0-2)	19.3%	28.1	57.8%	27.7	22.9%	70.6
P: No operational (0)//High promotions (3,4)//United States	16.8%	35.1	62.3%	32.8	20.4%	82.4
Q: Low operational (1)//Low promotions (0,1)//Up to college degree	13.2%	48.6	60.8%	28.7	26.0%	69.6
R: No operational (0)//Some promotion (0,1,2)//Some planning (2,3)	11.2%	36.6	65.4%	27.8	23.4%	59.6
S: More operational (2)//United States	10.3%	36.3	55.2%	16.6	34.5%	93.1
Correlation: Outcome proportion and time to outcome		−0.72		0.06		0.38

9.3   Overview: Start-up Activities Affecting Start-up Outcomes

Two different assessments of the effect of factors identified in the first 36 months of the start-up process on the outcomes reported after 72 months identify activities as having a greater impact. The results of the step-wise regression modeling and decision tree assessments are summarized in Table 9.4. The direction of the statistically significant beta coefficients are summarized in the regression model columns and the number of categories where the start-up activity was a factor in the decision tree assessment is summarized in the TREE columns.

Table 9.4: Factors with Impacts on Outcomes: Overview (without total acts).[1]

	Initial profits		Quit		Still active	
	Reg	Tree	Reg	Tree	Reg	Tree
Country (Not U.S.)	++	**/*	—	**/*	–	**/*
Promotion SU Activity	+++	**	–	***	-	**/*
Operation SU Activity	++	***	–		-	
Planning SU Activity		*	++	**	–	***
Innovation SU Activity	+		-			*
Funding SU Activity				*		
Infrastructure SU Activity	+	*	-			*
Growth orientation	-		+	*		
Technological emphasis				*	+	
Economic sector			-			
Educational attainment	-	*	-		+	
Work experience			-		+	
Start-up experience						
Age		*	-		+	
Gender						

Regression model standardized beta >0.19 = + + +/—; >0.10, <0.19 = ++/–; <0.10 +/-. First level tree = ***, 2nd level = **, 3rd level = *.

---

[1]Results of decision tree assessments on outcomes of quits and still active in the process provided in Appendix Tables D.1 and D.2.

As with the previous assessment, those ventures started outside the US were more likely to report profits, less likely to quit and less likely to continue active in the start-up process. Start-up activities and factors affecting outcomes can be summarized as follows:

- Initial efforts at promotion and developing an operational platform for delivering goods and services, both a factor in all six assessments, is associated with more nascent ventures in initial profits, less than quit, and less still active after 72 months.

- A focus on business planning, involved in five of six assessments, is associated with fewer new ventures reaching profitability, more that discontinue, and fewer that remain active after 72 months.

- A focus on infrastructure has a small positive impact on reaching initial profits, and a mixed impact on discontinuation or remaining active in the start-up process after 72 months.

- An emphasis on innovation has a small positive effect on reaching initial profits and may reduce the time spent in the start-up process after 72 months.

A number of personal and venture related factors seem to have some impact on different outcomes. More educational attainment seems to be associated with fewer ventures in profit or disengaged but more that are start-up active after 72 months. A technological emphasis may reduce those that quit and increase those still active. Those senior adults, over 55 years old, may be less likely to quit and stay active in the start-up process. An orientation toward growth ventures may reduce the transition to profit and increase disengagement. Ventures in business services may be less likely to quit. Work experience may reduce disengagements but increase those that remain active in the start-up process.

A summary of a similar assessment focusing on the time in the various processes is provided in Table 9.5. There are fewer consistent patterns, again reflecting the smaller number of cases involved in this analysis.

Table 9.5: Factors with Impacts on Time to Outcomes: Overview (without total acts).[2]

	Initial profits		Quit		Still active	
	Reg	Tree	Reg	Tree	Reg	Tree
Country (Not U.S.)	—	**/*	—	***/*	—	***
Promotion SU Activity	—	***/*				
Operation SU Activity	—					
Planning SU Activity				**	—	
Innovation SU Activity						
Funding SU Activity						
Infrastructure SU Activity	—			**	—	**
Growth orientation	++					
Technological emphasis	+					
Economic sector						
Educational attainment	+		+	*		
Work experience						
Start-up experience						
Age					++	
Gender						

Regression model standardized beta $>0.19 = +++/—$; >0.10, $<0.19 = ++/-$; $<0.10 +/-$. First level tree $= ****$, 2nd level $= ***$, 3rd level $= **$; 4th level $= *$.

Again, the national context has a major impact; outcomes are slower in the United States. Start-up activities with the major impact are:

- Promotion activity reduces the time to achieve initial profits and increases the time before a new venture is abandoned.

- An emphasis on operations and infrastructure also reduces the time to achieve initial profits.

- Growth orientation, a technological emphasis and more educated nascent entrepreneurs is associated with a longer time to reach profitability.

---

[2]Results of decision tree assessments on time to reach outcomes is provided in Appendix Tables D.3, D.4 and D.5.

- An emphasis on business planning or infrastructure reduced the time to disengagement and the time active in the start-up process.

- More educated nascent entrepreneurs take longer to reach initial profits or quit.

- Older nascent entrepreneurs may stay in the start-up process longer.

Few other factors seem to have a systematic impact.

10

Overview and Implications

This assessment has focused on the effect of different start-up activities on the outcome of the business creation process. Data from five longitudinal studies based on cohorts of representative samples of business creation in Australia, China, Sweden, and the United States was used to describe the process and outcomes. About one-third (34%) of the two thousand nascent ventures achieved profitability within 72 months, almost half (44%) had been terminated, and about one-in-five (22%) were still active in the business creation process. The average time to reach profitability was 26 months after entry into the business creation process, the average time to discontinue was 30 months, and those still active had been involved for an average of 58 months.

Harmonized measures of 19 start-up activities provide a comprehensive description of efforts to create a new business. All cohorts give similar emphasis to the activities, with serious thought about the new business eventually reported by all nascent entrepreneurs. There is considerable variation in the nature and sequence of start-up activities that are initiated, with development of a model or procedure for producing output, defining markets, creating a business plan, investing personal funds in the venture, and assembling supplies reported by over 80%

early in the process. Pursuing intellectual property rights, seeking funding and hiring employees are associated with less than one-quarter of the start-up efforts, later in the process.

Those nascent ventures associated with many activities early in the process are most likely to achieve profitability or be discontinued. A more leisurely implementation of start-up activities is associated with a long tenure in the start-up process.

Those nascent ventures achieving profitability are more likely to pursue many start-up activities, compared to those that remain active in the process or are disbanded. Analysis of relative impact was facilitated by creating six multi-item indices. Based on a factor analysis these were related to creating a public presence for the new firm, implementing operations, developing an organizational infrastructure, planning, developing outside funding, or working on a more complex initiatives. All indices were associated with differences in outcomes or times to reach the outcomes.

Identification of the most important factors affecting outcomes involved development of both linear additive models and interaction based models. Information about activities in the first 24 months was used to predict outcomes after 72 months. The total number of start-up activities initiated and the host country, or entrepreneurial context, had a major impact on both the outcomes and times to reach outcomes.

National context had a major effect on all outputs. Reaching profitability was more common in Australia, China, and Sweden than in the United States, and more nascent ventures discontinued or remained as active start-ups in the United States. Times to reach an outcome were also longer in the United States.

Once the impact of the volume of activities was excluded from the assessment, both the development of linear additive models and the decision tree analysis suggest that:

- Promotion of the business start-up activities (promoting output, public listings, business registration, and revenue) are strongly associated with reaching initial profits and not disengaging from the effort; it is associated with a reduction in continued participation in the start-up process.

- Operating business start-up activities (obtaining supplier credit, devoting full-time to the new venture, hiring employees) are strongly associated with reaching initial profits and not disengaging from the effort; it is associated with a reduced participation in the start-up process.

- Infrastructure development activities (acquire assets, purchasing supplies, investment of personal funds) are associated with reaching initial profits, discontinuation and reduced participation in the start-up process.

- Business plan development activities (defining markets, financial projections, business plan) are strongly associated with discontinuation of the effort and reduced participation in the start-up process; there is no effect in a multi-variate model on reaching initial profits.

- Innovation activities (developing a start-up team and intellectual property rights) are associated with reaching initial profits and reduced participation in the start-up process.

The total number of activities initiated in the first 24 months has a stronger association with outcomes than any other feature.

The major business characteristic that affected outcomes were a growth orientation, associated with fewer reaching profits and more quits. A strong focus on technology and the economic sector in which the firm would operate had little or no relationship to outcomes.

The personal background with the strongest association with the outcomes was educational attainment; those with college degrees or graduate training were less likely to reach profits or quit, but more likely to stay in the start-up process. These individuals may have been involved in more complicated, high potential nascent ventures. More work experience was associated with discontinuations and remaining in the start-up process. Experience with other start-ups was a factor in some interactive models after start-up activities were accounted for.

Personal characteristics, gender and age, had very little relationship to the outcomes. There was NO relationship associated with gender.

In only a few cases was age associated with outcomes, once the activities initiated were taken into account, older nascent entrepreneurs seemed to be more successful at achieving profits.

Predicting times to reach outcomes was not quite as successful, but all outcomes—profitability, disengagement, and still active in the process—were shorter for nascent ventures that initiated a large number of activities or were located in Australia, China and Sweden rather than in the United States. An emphasis on promotional, operational, and infrastructure activities tended to reduce the time to reach profitability. Nascent ventures with a growth orientation, a technological focus, initiated by those with college degrees or graduate experience tended to take longer to reach profitability. Initiation of planning and infrastructure activities is associated with less time to disengage from the start-up process; post high school education may increase the time before disengagement. A focus on planning and infrastructure activities tends to reduce the time active in the start-up process; those over 55 years old stay in the start-up process a little longer.

10.1   For Nascent Entrepreneurs

Perhaps the most significant implication from this assessment for those starting a new business is that anybody can do it.[1]

What you do is more important than who you are.

Once people get involved in the start-up process their personal background has little effect. Gender is not related to outcomes or time in process. Age may have a small effect that reflects the work experience and life situation of older individuals. Further, the sector in which the new business will compete is not associated with outcomes or time in process. The nature of the venture, an emphasis on growth or a focus on technological components, seems to have some impact. In combination with work and start-up experience this probably influences the

---

[1]This was the major conclusion of an earlier assessment with one cohort, the U.S. PSED I (Reynolds, 2007).

activities undertaken to implement a new firm. The effect of the activities on outcomes and timing is far more significant that these other features.

Two types of people may get involved in business creation.

- Committed nascent entrepreneurs who have made a decision that creating a new firm is an important career opportunity.

- Exploratory nascent entrepreneurs seem to be attracted to the idea of firm creation, but are not quite ready to go "all in."

Findings from the assessment may help those in both categories.

Those serious about a new career should expect it to take 12-24 months to determine if the nascent venture will achieve profitability. Only in rare cases will this be obvious in the first 6 months. Some start-up activities can help provide an early indication of the venture's potential. Efforts to promote the new venture and engage with potential customers can clarify the attraction of the output. Efforts to develop an organization to deliver the goods or services, which may require assembling the components for the infrastructure, may provide timely information on expected costs and the appropriate balance among critical components. This implication is consistent with the focus of the NSF sponsored I-Corp training, reflecting the recommended agenda proposed by the "lean start-up" strategy.[2]

Business planning may clarify the investment required to implement a new firm as well shorted the time required to reach an outcome, but without information provided by actually doing a start-up and engaging with customers it may not facilitate profitability. Business planning may clarify the potential of the start-up venture sooner rather than later.

The situation of exploratory nascent entrepreneurs is not well defined. Perhaps because their current career situation has some advantages or they have not fully develop their new business idea they initiate start-up activities at a more relaxed pace and can take quite a while

---

[2]Osterwalder and Pigneur (2013); Reiss (2011); National Science Foundation (2016).

to make a decision about business creation. For this group, preparing a business plan seems to shorten the time they are in "start-up limbo."

10.2   For Policy Makers

There are many good reasons to promote business creation. The development of new firms is a two stage process. First, individuals or teams must decide to become involved in business creation and enter the business creation process. Second, start up teams must take appropriate steps such that a nascent venture will achieve profitability and be an established part of the economy.

Globally, there is substantial diversity in participation in business creation, from 2 per 100 adults to over 30 per hundred adults.[3] If the participation is below 5 per 100 adults, it may be appropriate to implement policies to increase participation. It is, however, very difficult to encourage major changes in business creation, particularly in a short period of time.[4] Reducing the costs and increasing the potential for success of those in the firm creation process may attract more participants.

Any effort to create a new business absorbs time and money. The amount of time and money absorbed by nascent ventures that do not reach profits is substantial, a social cost that offsets the benefits provided by viable new firms. While there is a substantial public benefit from the continuous emergence of new firms, there is a substantial social cost to maintaining an active entrepreneurial sector.

The sunk cost associated with nascent ventures that will not become viable will be reduced if their lack of potential is determined sooner rather than later. These nascent entrepreneurs may then pursue other career options, perhaps work or starting a different new firm. The resources encumbered by these nascent ventures can be redeployed for other, perhaps more profitable, uses. In most countries the majority of nascent ventures do not reach profitability, so a focus on an early decision can do much to reduce the social cost of the entrepreneurial

---

[3]This diversity and the relationship to personal income status is discussed in some detail in a cross national analysis (Reynolds, 2012).

[4]Reynolds (2015a).

engine. Business planning can make a major contribution to providing an early determination of an appropriate outcome.

This assessment suggest that an emphasis on promotion of a new venture, developing the operational capacity to deliver the good or service and implementing an infrastructure for the venture all lead to acquiring profit sooner rather than later. While the pursuit of funding may be required to implement some of these activities, it is not, by itself, a major factor affecting the outcome.

Time to reach initial profits may take longer for nascent ventures that are based on some advanced technology. It may be a little quicker for ventures in business or consumer services, compared to those in extractive or transformation, which includes construction, manufacturing, transportation and wholesale.

There are a range of public policies and procedures designed to encourage business creation, from adjustments in the tax laws and special programs for new businesses to adjustments in the educational programs at all levels. The major implication from this assessment is that all these efforts would benefit from reflecting a realistic assessment of the potential for success, the time required to reach an outcome, and an emphasis on doing things that will connect the venture to the potential customers. Such an emphasis should complement to the current heavy focus on developing outside funding.

10.3 For Understanding of Business Creation

This assessment has identified a number of factors related to the business creation process. Two different procedures identified factors associated with the outcomes and time to reach the outcomes. One procedure involved the development of linear additive models that emerged from a step-wise regression analysis. The other led to models that identified the interaction among start-up factors that would predict outcomes. In both cases inferences about the importance of initial factors relied on statistically significant effects identified in the assessments. This has been a major advancement in understanding firm creation, made possible by a unique longitudinal data set.

Perhaps the first contribution has been to place business planning, as a start-up activity, in a broader context. If the only start-up activity that is considered in relation to outcomes is business planning, it will clearly be identified as a statistically significant factor. But in such assessments business planning will be an indicator of all start-up activities. The results can be misleading, as it is the other activities that seem to facilitate profitability, not business planning per se.

If it was possible to implement controlled experiments with the start-up process by randomly assigning different activities to the nascent ventures, it would be possible to have strong confidence in the impact on outcomes. This was not possible and tracking the decisions to pursue different activities in a representative sample was the only feasible option. It is possible that unmeasured features of the start-up team, situation, or the venture itself are correlated with the decisions to pursue different activities. While some strategies have been developed to "correct for endogeneity" they have not been utilized in this analysis.[5]

A more complete understanding of the firm creation process would result from two further assessments. First, understanding those factors that affect the start-up activities pursued in the creation of a new firm.[6] It would amount to identifying the critical relationships in Figure 10.1. This presents a model with five categories of variables, all expected to affect the outcomes and time to reach the outcomes. The national context, economic sector, background of the start-up team, and major features of the nascent venture are expected to affect both start-up activities and outcomes. The start-up activities are considered intervening variables that will affect the outcomes.

A number of processes affecting the implementation of start-up activities would be represented by variables not available in the current five cohort data set. Such as details about the nature of the specific market sectors in which the new venture would complete, the availability of resources (managerial talent, trained employees, supplies and

---

[5]Hamilton and Nickerson (2003); Samadeni, Withers, and Certo (2014).

[6]One assessment has considered the effect of a founding teams network structure influences initiating founding activities (Kreiser, Patel, and Fiet, 2013).

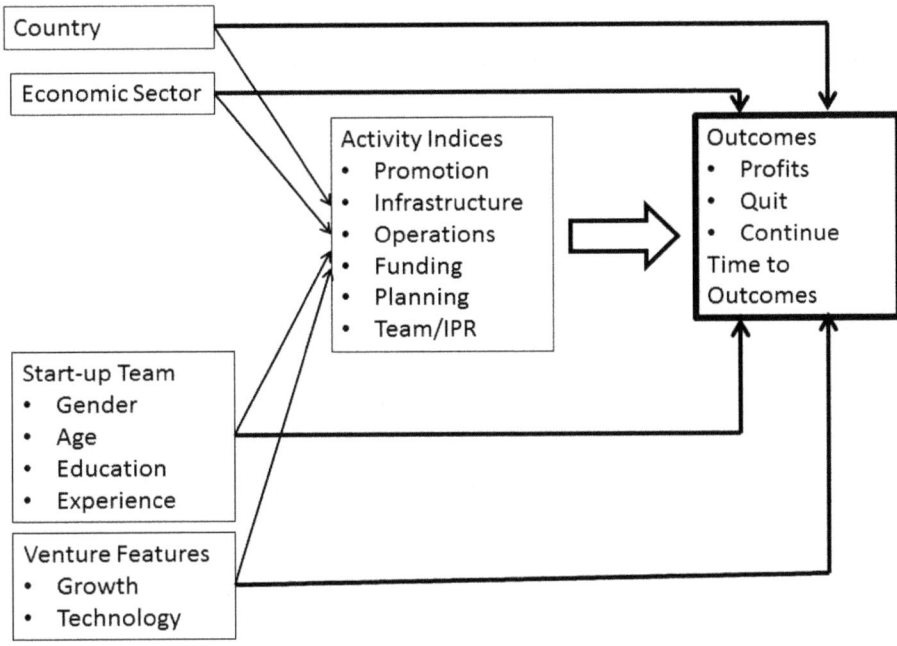

Figure 10.1: Model of Factors Affecting Start-up Activities and Outcomes.

materials, capital assets, external funding), general economic conditions that may affect the demand for the goods or services to be provided by the new firm, or the nature of the political and cultural context in which business creation takes place.

The second assessment would be a more complete description of how the nascent entrepreneur or start-up team pursued the business opportunity. This would involve more details about the development of the business idea and selection of actions to be taken to implement the new firm. It may require a personal visit and face-to-face interviews with the individuals responsible for implementing the new firm. Given that the ventures represented by the current five-cohort data set were identified up to 10 years ago, a new representative sample of nascent ventures should probably be developed. Site visits and personal interviews could then be implemented early in the process with ventures that would eventually reach profitability as well as those that would eventually be abandoned. While there are a multitude of case studies of business creation, most are retrospective accounts or selected for instructional purposes to demonstrate some issue associated with business creation. Very few reflect a selection of cases that represent a known population of nascent ventures. Case studies reflecting a representative sample could provide major contributions to understanding the firm creation process.

This assessment has provided a range of new information about business creation and the start-up process based on representative samples of nascent ventures. Additional efforts would make important contributions by expanding details about the process and could improve both predictive precision and a sense of understanding. The importance of business creation to economic growth and personal careers clearly justifies the additional effort.

Appendices

A

Aggregation, Harmonization of Five PSED Cohorts

An overview of the five cohorts from four countries is provided in Table A.1.[1] The successive rows represent the various stages in gathering and processing the data. Each project involved three stages. The initial screening of a representative sample of the adult population, which included the entire country in the United States, Australia, and Sweden and eight major cities selected to represent four major regions of China. A total of 175 thousand adults were screened in the five projects and 6,024 candidates for the first detailed interview were identified.

Once those active in business creation were identified in the screening interview, the second phase was completion of detailed set of questions about their effort, often in a separate session and sometimes with a different survey staff. As can be seen in Table 5.1, 3,893 of the candidates completed the initial wave 1 interviews which involved those actions taken to implement the new firm, the nature of the start-up team, possible sources of financial support, aspirations for the new firm, per-

---

[1] Complete details of the processing to harmonize the five cohorts is available in Reynolds et al. (2016). Information about the surveys completed by each project are available from the project websites or similar sources.

Table A.1: Cohort Development Overview: Five Projects.

	US PSED I	US PSED II	AU-CAUSEE	SE-PSED	CH-PSED	Total
Screening Initiated	Jul 98	Oct 05	Apr 07	Apr 98	Jul 09	
Screening Completed	Jan 00	Jan 06	Apr 08	Oct 98	Aug 09	
Nascent screening sample	62,612	31,845	30,105	30,427	20,998	175,987
Screening identified nascents	1,492	1,587	1,010	961	974	6,024
Completed Wave 1 interview	830	1,214	625	623	601	3,893
One or more follow-up interviews	695	1,110	524	584	321	3,441
Active nascent entrepreneurs	665	902	546	395	409	3,002
1 Mth: Active nascents & follow-up	569	860	439	382	263	2,513
12 Mth: Active nascents & follow-up	565	856	439	382	263	2,505
24 Mth: Active nascents & follow-up	549	845	432	362	247	2,435
36 Mth: Active nascents & follow-up	541	818	411	349	232	2,351
48 Mth: Active nascents & follow-up	524	801	402	339	220	2,286
60 Mth: Active nascents & follow-up	496	782	396	331	218	2.225
72 Mth: Active nascents & follow-up	419	712	379	330	217	2,057

sonal background and other topics, which differed among projects. The number of follow-up interviews varied, with two completed in China, three in US-PSED I, four in the CAUSEE (Australian) effort, and five in the US PSED II and Swedish projects. A total of 3,441 completed one or more follow-up interviews, critical for obtaining information on the outcomes of the effort.

However, when these 3,441 cases were examined in detail it became apparent some were not active in the initial stages of firm creation. A number reported profits before the initial screening and others were not very involved in business creation. Those that qualified as actively involved with nascent ventures in the pre-profit stage were 3,002, of which one or more follow-up interviews were completed with 2,541. However, the number completing follow-up interviews declines over time with in all five projects. As a result, of the 3,317 only 2,050 or so meet the criteria for active nascent entrepreneurs at entry into the process cases with follow-up data at 72 months after entry. Given fractional case weights and the occasional missing data for some variables, this number may vary from one assessment to another.

There were two stages to the development of case weights. First the weights developed for each case in the screening sample, created so the screening sample would have the same characteristics as the total adult population, were attached to each nascent venture case. As those start-ups to be implemented by a larger team were more likely to be represented in a screening to locate team members, the population case weights were adjusted to reduce the impact of those nascent ventures being implemented by larger start-up teams. The second stage was to divide the respondent weight by the number of humans expected to own part of the business. The final adjustment was to re-center the weights so the average value was one; the sum of the weights would then equal the sum of the cases. This ensures that the inferences about statistical significance, and analysis procedures that utilize such criteria, are not biased.

One important feature of the consolidated data set is that 56% of the cases are from the United States, 18% from Australia, 15% from Sweden, and 10% from China. Substantial national influences on business creation may affect some features of the business creation process. Country of context is taken into account in most of the assessments.

The implementation and timing of 19 start-up activities was harmonized across all five cohorts. Eighteen activities, excluding initial serious thought about starting a business, were used to identify the earlier of two activities that occurred within a 12 month period. This was considered the date of entry into the process and it occurred, on average, 17 months before the initial detailed interview.[2] The transition to a new firm was dated as the first of three or six months when monthly revenue covered all expenses and financial support of the owners. Date of disengagement was based on the respondents' reports of no further work on the start-up. Those ventures that did not report initial profits or disengagement were considered to be still active in the start-up process; the date of the last follow-up interview was used as the last date the venture was active in the start-up process.

A full report on the consolidated data set is available on Research Gate (Reynolds et al., 2016), as well as data files in SPSS, SYSTAT, and SAS.

---

[2]The average lag ranged from 12 months for China to 24 months for U.S. PSED I.

B

Inter-correlation Among Start-up Activities Initiate in First 24 Months

Table B.1: Inter-correlation among Start-up Activities Reported in First 24 Months.

GETFNDAW RECEIVED OUTSIDE FINANCING

EIN____AW APPLY FOR BUSINESS REGISTRATION

BUSPLNAW DEVELOP BUSINESS PLAN

SUTEAMAW ORGANIZE START-UP TEAM

MODEL_AW DEVELOP MODEL, PROTOTYPE

PROMOTAW PROMOTING GOODS, SERVICES

PATENTAW APPLY PATENT, COPYRIGHT, TRADEMARK

PURCHAAW PURCHASED SUPPLIES, MATERIAL, INVENT

LEASE_AW LEASED, PURCHASED CAPITAL ASSETS

DFNMKTAW BEGAN DEFINING MARKETS

FINPRJAW DEVELOP FINANCIAL PROJECTIONS

ONINVAW1 TM MBR 1 (R) INVESTED OWN MONEY

ASKFNDAW ASKED FOR OUTSIDE FUNDING

SUPCRDAW ASKED FOR SUPPLIER CREDIT

FTWK_AW1 TM MBR 1 DEVOTED FULL TIME

HIRE___AW INITIAL EMPLOYEE HIRED

SALES_AW INITIAL SALES, REVENUE, INCOME

PHLISTAW INITIAL DEDICATED PHONE LINE

THINK_AW SERIOUS THOUGHT BUS IDEA

	THINK_AW	PHLISTAW	SALES_AW	HIRE__AW	FTWK_AW1	SUPCRDAW	ASKFNDAW	ONINVAW	FINPRJAW
THINK_AW	1.00								
Sig. (2-tailed)									
PHLISTAW	0.17	1.00							
Sig. (2-tailed)	0.00								
SALES_AW	0.15	0.31	1.00						
Sig. (2-tailed)	0.00	0.00							
HIRE__AW	0.04	0.16	0.22	1.00					
Sig. (2-tailed)	0.05	0.00	0.00						
FTWK_AW1	0.04	0.15	0.18	0.23	1.00				
Sig. (2-tailed)	0.03	0.00	0.00	0.00					
SUPCRDAW	0.12	0.12	0.19	0.27	0.23	1.00			
Sig. (2-tailed)	0.00	0.00	0.00	0.00	0.00				
ASKFNDAW	-0.02	-0.01	0.04	0.18	0.12	0.16	1.00		
Sig. (2-tailed)	0.35	0.72	0.06	0.00	0.00	0.00			
ONINVAW	0.25	0.07	0.19	0.02	0.09	0.12	0.00	1.00	
Sig. (2-tailed)	0.00	0.00	0.00	0.29	0.00	0.00	0.89		
FINPRJAW	-0.05	0.07	0.13	0.21	0.18	0.22	0.20	0.03	1.00
Sig. (2-tailed)	0.02	0.00	0.00	0.00	0.00	0.00	0.00	0.16	

(Continued)

Table B.1: (*Continued*)

	THINK_AW SERIOUS THOUGHT BUS IDEA	PHLISTAW INITIAL DEDICATED PHONE LINE	SALES_AW INITIAL SALES, REVENUE, INCOME	HIRE___AW INITIAL EMPLOYEE HIRED	FTWK_AW1 TM MBR 1 DEVOTED FULL TIME	SUPCRDAW ASKED FOR SUPPLIER CREDIT	ASKFNDAW ASKED FOR OUTSIDE FUNDING	ONINVAW1 TM MBR 1 (R) INVESTED OWN MONEY	FINPRJAW DEVELOP FINANCIAL PROJECTIONS	DFNMKTAW BEGAN DEFINING MARKETS	LEASE_AW LEASED, PURCHASED CAPITAL ASSETS	PURCHAAW PURCHASED SUPPLIES, MATERIAL, INVENT	PATENTAW APPLY PATENT, COPYRIGHT, TRADEMARK	PROMOTAW PROMOTING GOODS, SERVICES	MODEL_AW DEVELOP MODEL, PROTOTYPE	SUTEAMAW ORGANIZE START-UP TEAM	BUSPLNAW DEVELOP BUSINESS PLAN	EIN____AW APPLY FOR BUSINESS REGISTRATION	GETFNDAW RECEIVED OUTSIDE FINANCING
DFNMKTAW	0.04	0.00	0.04	0.06	0.08	0.14	0.08	0.07	0.24	1.00									
Sig. (2-tailed)	0.05	0.98	0.06	0.00	0.00	0.00	0.00	0.00	0.00										
LEASE_AW	0.15	0.21	0.28	0.23	0.14	0.16	0.08	0.18	0.08	0.08	1.00								
Sig. (2-tailed)	0.00	0.00	0.00	0.00	0.00	0.00	0.00	0.00	0.00	0.00									
PURCHAAW	0.18	0.14	0.28	0.13	0.05	0.19	0.04	0.25	0.02	0.08	0.32	1.00							
Sig. (2-tailed)	0.00	0.00	0.00	0.00	0.01	0.00	0.07	0.00	0.31	0.00	0.00								
PATENTAW	-0.05	0.00	-0.01	0.08	0.06	0.08	0.06	-0.01	0.10	0.09	-0.03	-0.02	1.00						
Sig. (2-tailed)	0.02	0.92	0.57	0.00	0.00	0.00	0.00	0.69	0.00	0.00	0.17	0.23							
PROMOTAW	0.10	0.23	0.33	0.15	0.15	0.19	0.11	0.14	0.20	0.26	0.19	0.27	0.09	1.00					
Sig. (2-tailed)	0.00	0.00	0.00	0.00	0.00	0.00	0.00	0.00	0.00	0.00	0.00	0.00	0.00						
MODEL_AW	0.03	0.06	0.15	0.00	-0.03	-0.02	0.01	0.04	-0.03	0.05	0.09	0.18	0.06	0.10	1.00				
Sig. (2-tailed)	0.17	0.00	0.00	0.91	0.10	0.26	0.75	0.04	0.16	0.01	0.00	0.00	0.00	0.00					
SUTEAMAW	-0.09	-0.07	0.00	0.12	0.10	0.11	0.17	0.02	0.16	0.14	0.04	0.00	0.17	0.10	0.05	1.00			
Sig. (2-tailed)	0.00	0.00	0.96	0.00	0.00	0.00	0.00	0.32	0.00	0.00	0.05	0.88	0.00	0.00	0.01				
BUSPLNAW	-0.02	0.05	0.03	0.08	0.09	0.09	0.14	0.06	0.32	0.16	0.01	-0.02	0.06	0.14	-0.02	0.13	1.00		
Sig. (2-tailed)	0.42	0.01	0.17	0.00	0.00	0.00	0.00	0.01	0.00	0.00	0.65	0.41	0.00	0.00	0.31	0.00			
EIN____AW	-0.02	0.12	0.28	0.17	0.17	0.17	0.19	0.13	0.18	0.10	0.17	0.08	0.08	0.21	0.03	0.13	0.10	1.00	
Sig. (2-tailed)	0.24	0.00	0.00	0.00	0.00	0.00	0.00	0.00	0.00	0.00	0.00	0.00	0.00	0.00	0.10	0.00	0.00		
GETFNDAW	0.07	0.14	0.15	0.17	0.12	0.19	0.51	0.02	0.16	0.09	0.13	0.09	-0.02	0.14	0.02	0.03	0.10	0.15	1.00
Sig. (2-tailed)	0.00	0.00	0.00	0.00	0.00	0.00	0.00	0.39	0.00	0.00	0.00	0.00	0.27	0.00	0.31	0.14	0.00	0.00	

C

Decision Tree Interactive Models: All Independent Variables

Table C.1: Interactive Models: Predicting Quits –Decision Tree Analysis.

Group	1st level	2nd level	3rd level	% Quit	Group % all	Number active	% Total sample	Group count
A	2-11 SU Acts	Some planning(2,3)	China, Sweden, U.S.	62.1%	55.3%	495	40.0%	797
B	12-18 SU Acts	U.S.	Growth preference (1)	56.1%	4.1%	37	3.3%	66
C	2-11 SU Acts	Lowplanning (1)	Up to college degree	11.9%	17.8%	159	17.8%	354
D	2-11 SU Acts	Noplanning (0)	No tech emphasis (0)	11.3%	4.4%	39	4.4%	88
E	2-11 SU Acts	Some planning (2,3)	Australia	36.3%	8.7%	78	10.8%	215
F	12-18 SU Acts	U.S.	No growth (0)	25.8%	4.7%	42	8.2%	163
G	2-11 SU Acts	Lowplanning (1)	Graduate education	21.4%	1.0%	9	2.1%	42
H	2-11 SU Acts	Noplanning (0)	Tech emphasis (1,2,3)	18.5%	1.9%	17	4.6%	92
I	12-18 SU Acts	AU, CH, SE		10.9%	2.1%	19	8.7%	174
				45.0%	100.0%	895	100.0%	1991

Table C.2: Interactive Models: Predicting Active Start-ups –Decision Tree Analysis.

Group	1st level	2nd level	3rd level	% SU Active	Group % all	Number active	% Total sample	Group count
A	6-8 SU Acts	Australia	College degree	58.8%	4.6%	20	1.7%	34
B	2-5 SU Acts	Low planning (0,1)	No innovation (0)	54.8%	27.4%	120	11.0%	219
C	2-5 SU Acts	Some planning (2,3)	One+ other start-ups	36.2%	3.9%	17	2.4%	47
D	6-8 SU Acts	Australia	Graduate experience	35.4%	7.8%	34	4.8%	96
E	9-11 SU Acts	AU, SE, U.S.	Australia	29.5%	7.1%	31	5.3%	105
F	6-8 SU Acts	CH, SE, U.S.	21+ Yrs work experience	29.5%	8.2%	36	6.1%	122
G	6-8 SU Acts	CH, SE, U.S.	0-5 Yrs work experience	17.3%	6.4%	28	7.7%	153
H	9-11 SU Acts	AU, SE, U.S.	Sweden, U.S.	18.2%	17.4%	76	21.0%	418
I	12-18 SU Acts	AU, SE, U.S.	Some funding effort (0,1)	14.7%	7.8%	34	11.6%	231
J	2-5 SU Acts	Low planning (0,1)	Some Innovation (1,2)	12.5%	1.1%	5	2.0%	40
K	2-5 SU Acts	Some planning (2,3)	First start-up	10.9%	2.5%	11	5.1%	101
L	6-8 SU Acts	CH, SE, U.S.	6-20 Yrs work experience	10.4%	4.3%	19	9.2%	183
M	12-18 SU Acts	AU, SE, U.S.	High funding support (2)	6.0%	1.6%	7	5.8%	116
N	9-11 SU Acts	China		0.0%	0.0%	0	3.5%	70
O	12-18 SU Acts	China		0.0%	0.0%	0	2.8%	56
				22.0%	100.0%	438	100.0%	1991

Table C.3: Interactive Models: Predicting Time to Profits –Decision Tree Analysis.

Group	1st level	2nd level	3rd level	Mths	Group % all	Number active
A	3-5 SU Acts			42.9	8.5%	56
B	6-8 SU Acts	45-54 Yrs old		35.0	4.4%	29
C	9-11 SU Acts	US		30.4	12.3%	81
D	6-8 SU Acts	18-44, 55-64 Yrs old	Male	29.1	10.0%	66
E	9-11 SU Acts	AU, CH, SE	Funding effort (1,2)	22.9	4.3%	28
F	6-8 SU Acts	18-44, 55-64 Yrs old	Female	21.6	5.8%	38
G	12-18 SU Acts	US	18-34, 45-64 Yrs old	21.4	11.7%	77
H	12-18 SU Acts	AU, CH, SE	Australia	18.4	5.3%	35
I	12-18 SU Acts	US	35-44 Yrs old	16.6	6.5%	43
J	9-11 SU Acts	AU, CH, SE	No funding effort (0)	13.6	14.6%	96
K	12-18 SU Acts	AU, CH, SE	China, Sweden	12.7	16.6%	109
				22.7	100.0%	658

Table C.4: Interactive Models: Predicting Time to Quits –Decision Tree Analysis.

Group	1st level	2nd level	3rd level	Mths	Group % all	Number active
A	US			30.0	62.2%	522
B	AU, CH, SE	Little planning (0,1)		25.6	6.8%	57
C	AU, CH, SE	High planning (3)	Extrac, Transofma, Buss Services	23.8	6.3%	53
D	AU, CH, SE	Some planning (2)	35-44 Yrs old	22.3	3.7%	31
E	AU, CH, SE	High planning (3)	Consumer services	19.0	11.2%	94
K	AU, CH, SE	Some planning (2)	18-34, 45-64 Yrs old	15.1	9.8%	82
				26.3	100.0%	839

Table C.5: Interactive Models: Predicting Time as Active Start-up –Decision Tree Analysis.

Group	1st level	2nd level	3rd level	Mths	Group % all	Number active
A	China, Sweden, U.S.	Little infrastructure (0,1)		105.3	19.9%	63
B	China, Sweden, U.S.	More infrastructure (2,3)		82.1	60.1%	190
C	Australia			44.5	19.9%	63
				79.3	100.0%	316

D

Decision Tree Interactive Models: All Independent Variable Except Total Start-up Activity

Table D.1: Interactive Models: Predicting Quits – Decision Tree Analysis (without total activity).

Group	1st level	2nd level	3rd level	% Active	Group % all	Number active	% Total sample	Group count
A	No promotions (0)	Some planning (2,3)	Low tech emphasis	79.6%	12.6%	113	7.1%	142
B	Some promotion (1,2)	Some planning (2,3)	United States	68.3%	21.2%	190	14.0%	278
C	High promotions (3)	United States	High growth	63.9%	7.7%	69	5.4%	108
D	No promotions (0)	Some planning (2,3)	Some tech emphasis	56.4%	2.5%	22	2.0%	39
E	No promotions (0)	Little planning (1)		48.9%	5.1%	46	4.7%	94
F	Some promotion (1,2)	Low planning (0,1)	No technology	45.5%	6.8%	61	6.7%	134
G	Some promotion (1,2)	Some planning (2,3)	AU, CH, SE	45.1%	14.9%	133	14.8%	295
H	High promotions (3)	United States	Low growth	39.2%	15.6%	140	17.9%	357
I	No promotions (0)	No planning (0)		27.8%	1.1%	10	1.8%	36
J	Some promotion (1,2)	Low planning (0,1)	Some tech emphasis	27.7%	4.9%	44	8.0%	159
K	High promotions (3)	AU, CH, SE	No funding activity (0)	24.6%	6.9%	62	12.7%	252
L	High promotions (3)	AU, CH, SE	Funding emphasis (1,2)	5.2%	0.6%	5	4.9%	97
				45.0%	99.9%	895	100.0%	1991

Table D.2: Interactive Models: Predicting Active Start-ups –Decision Tree Analysis (without total activity).

Group	1st level	2nd level	3rd level	% Active	Group % all	Number active	% Total sample	Group count
A	No planning (0)	Low promotion (0,1)		55.7%	12.3%	54	4.9%	97
B	Low planning (1)	Some promotion (2,3)	Low infrastructure (0,1)	48.8%	4.8%	21	2.2%	43
C	Low planning (1)	Low promotion (0,1)	No innovation (0)	46.4%	14.8%	65	7.0%	140
D	Some planning (2,3)	Australia	Some promotion (0,1,2)	45.6%	14.2%	62	6.8%	136
E	No planning (0)	Some promotion (2,3,4)		29.8%	5.7%	25	4.2%	84
F	Low planning (1)	Some promotion (2,3)	Some infrastructure (2,3)	21.3%	6.8%	30	7.1%	141
G	Low planning (1)	Low promotion (0,1)	Some innovation (1,2)	17.0%	1.8%	8	2.4%	47
H	Some planning (2,3)	Australia	High promotion (3,4)	16.9%	4.8%	21	6.2%	124
I	Some planning (2,3)	CH, SE, US	Sweden, US	15.2%	33.1%	145	47.8%	951
J	Low planning (1)	Highest promotion (4)		5.1%	0.5%	2	2.0%	39
K	Some planning (2,3)	CH, SE, US	China	2.6%	1.1%	5	9.5%	189
				22.0%	99.9%	438	100.1%	1991

Table D.3: Interactive Models: Predicting Time to Profits –Decision Tree Analysis (without total activity).

Group	1st level	2nd level	3rd level	Mths	Group % all	Number active
A	No promotion (0)			53.3	6.9%	48
B	Low promotion (1)			41.6	13.6%	95
C	Some promotion (2)	US		35.1	9.6%	67
D	High promotion (3,4)	US	High promotion (3)	31.0	11.9%	83
E	High promotion (3,4)	US	Maximum promotion (4)	22.1	14.3%	100
F	High promotion (3,4)	AU, CH, SE	Australia	21.8	12.7%	89
G	Some promotion (2)	AU, CH, SE	China, Sweden	18.7	9.7%	68
H	High promotion (3,4)	AU, CH, SE	No funding effort (0)	12.5	21.3%	149
				26.7	100.0%	699

Table D.4: Interactive Models: Predicting Time to Quits –Decision Tree Analysis (without total activity).

Group	1st level	2nd level	3rd level	Mths	Group % all	Number active
A	US	No infrastructure (0)		50.6	3.9%	37
B	US	Some infrastructure (1,2,3)	Post High school education	34.6	23.4%	220
C	AU, CH, SE	Little planning (0,1)		34.4	7.2%	68
D	US	Some infrastructure (1,2,3)	High school degree	30.5	36.0%	339
E	AU, CH, SE	Some planning (2,3)	Sweden	23.9	11.5%	108
f	AU, CH, SE	Some planning (2,3)	Australia, China	18.5	18.0%	170
				29.6	100.0%	942

Table D.5: Interactive Models: Predicting Time as Active Start-up –Decision Tree Analysis (without total activity).

Group	1st v	2nd level	3rd level	Mths	Group % all	Number active
A	CH, SE, US	Little infrastructure (0,1)		107.4	20.3%	50
B	CH, SE, US	Some infrastructure (2,3)		81.0	57.7%	142
C	Australia			40.3	22.0%	54
				77.4	100.0%	246

References

Barnard, C. I. (1951). *The Functions of the Executive*. Cambridge, MA: Harvard U. Press.

Bergmann, H. and U. Stephan (2012). Moving on from nascent entrepreneurship: measuring cross-national differences in the transition to new business ownership. *Small Business Economics 41*, 945–959.

Brinckmann, J., D. Grichnik, and D. Kapsa (2010). Should entrepreneurs plan or just storm the castle? A meta-analysis on contextual factors impacting the business planning-performance relationship in small firms. *Journal of Business Venturing 25*, 24–40.

Burke, A., S. Fraser, and F. J. Greene (2010). The Multiple Effects of Business Planning on New Venture Performance. *Journal of Management Studies 47*(3), 391–415.

Bush, C. G., T. S. Manolova, and L. F. Edelman (2008). Properties of Emerging Organizations: An empirical test. *Journal of Business Venturing 23*, 547–566.

Campbell, J. R. and M. D. Nardi (2009). A conversation with 590 Nascent Entrepreneurs. *Annals of Finance 5*, 313–340.

Chwolka, A. and M. G. Raith (2012). The value of business planning before start-up-A decision-theoretical perspective. *Journal of Business Venturing 27*, 385–399.

Davidsson, P. (2015). Data replication and extension: A commentary. *Journal of Business Venturing Insights 3*, 12–15.

121

Davidsson, P. and S. R. Gordon (2012). Panel studies of new venture creation: a methods-focused review and suggestion for future research. *Small Business Economics 39*, 853–876.

Delmar, F. (2015a). A response to Honig and Samuelsson. *Journal of Business Venturing Insights 3*, 1–4.

Delmar, F. (2015b). When the dust had settled: A final note on replication. *Journal of Business Venturing Insights 4*, 20–21.

Delmar, F. and P. Davidsson (2000). Where do they come from? Prevalence and characteristics of nascent entrepreneurs. *Entrepreneurship & Regional Development 12*(1), 1–23.

Delmar, F. and S. Shane (2003). Does Business Planning Facilitate the Development of New Ventures. *Strategic Management Journal 24*, 1165–1185.

Delmar, F. and S. Shane (2004). Legitimating first: organizing activities and the survival of new ventures. *Journal of Business Venturing 19*, 385–410.

Frid, C. (2015). *Publications Based on the Panel Study of Entrepreneurial Dynamics.* Ann Arbor: MI: University of Michigan, PSED website ('www.psed.isr.umich').

Gartner, W. B., N. M. Carter, and P. D. Reynolds (2004). Business Start-up Activities. In W. B. Gartner et al (Ed.), *Handbook of Entrepreneurial Dynamics: The Process of Business Creation*, Chapter 26, pp. 285–298. Thousand Oaks, CA: Sage.

Gartner, W. B. and K. G. Shaver (2012). Nascent entrepreneurship panel studies: progress and challenges. *Small Business Economics 39*, 659–665.

Gatewood, E. J., K. G. Shaver, and W. B. Gartner (1995). A Longitudinal Study of Cognitive Factors Influencing Start-up Behaviors and Success at Venture Creation. *Journal of Business Venturing 10*, 371–391.

Gielnik, M. M., S. Barabas, M. Frese, R. Namatovu-Dawa, F. A. Scholz, J. R. Metzger, and T. Walter (2014). A Temporal analysis of how entrepreneurial goal intentions, positive fantasies, and action planning affect starting a new venture when the effects wear off. *Journal of Business Venturing 29*, 755–772.

Hamilton, B. H. and J. A. Nickerson (2003). Correcting for endogeneity in strategic management research. *Strategic Organization 1*(1), 51–78.

Honig, B. and T. Karlsson (2004). Institutional Forces and the Written Business Plan. *Journal of Management 30*(1), 29–48.

Honig, B. and M. Samuelsson (2014). Data replication and extension: A Study of business planning and venture-level performance. *Journal of Business Venturing Insights 1-2*, 18–25.

Honig, B. and M. Samuelsson (2015). Replication in entrepreneurship research: a further response to Delmar. *Journal of Business Venturing Insights 13*, 30–34.

Hopp, C. and R. Sonderegger (2015). Understanding the dynamics of Nascent entrepreneurship—Prestart-Up experience, Intentions and Entrepreneurial Success. *Journal of Small Business Management 53*(4), 1076–1096.

Katz, J. and W. B. Gartner (1988). Properties of emerging organizations. *Academy of Management Review 13*(3), 429–441.

Kessler, A. and H. Frank (2009). Nascent Entrepreneurship in a Longitudinal Perspective: The Impact of Person, Environment, Resources and the Founding Process on the Decision to Start Business Activities. *International Small Business Journal 27*(6), 720–742.

Kreiser, P. M., P. C. Patel, and J. O. Fiet (2013). The Influence of Changes in Social Capital on Firm-Founding Activities. *Entrepreneurship Theory and Practice,* May, 539–567.

Lawless, M. (2014). Age or size? Contributions to job creation. *Small Business Economics 42*, 815–830.

Liao, J. and W. B. Gartner (2006). The Effects of Pre-venture Plan Timing and Perceived Environmental Uncertainty on the Persistence of Emerging Firms. *Small Business Economics 27*, 23–40.

Liao, J. and H. Welsch (2008). Patterns of venture gestation process: Exploring the differences between tech and non-tech nascent entrepreneurs. *Journal of High Technology Management Research 19*, 103–113.

Liao, J., H. Welsch, and W.-L. Tan (2005). Venture gestation pathes of nascent entrepreneurs: Exploring the temporal patterns. *Journal of High Technology Management Research 16*, 1–22.

Lichtenstein, B. B., N. M. Carter, K. J. Dooley, and W. B. Gartner (2007). Complexity dynamics of nascent entrepreneurship. *Journal of Business Venturing 22*, 236–261.

Meyer, M., D. Libaers, B. Thijs, K. Grant, W. Glanzel, and K. Debackere (2014). Origin and emergence of entrepreneurship as a research field. *Scientometrics 98*, 473–485.

Mueller, S., T. Volery, and B. von Siemens (2012). What do entrepreneurs actually do? An Observational Study of Entrepreneurs Everyday Behavior in the Start-up and Growth Stages. *Entrepreneurship Theory and Practice,* September, 995–1017.

National Science Foundation (2016). NSF Innovation Crops., www.nsf.gov/ news/special_reports/i_corps.

Osterwalder, A. and Y. Pigneur (2013). *Business Model Generation: A Handbook for Visionaries, Game Changers, and Challengers.* New York: Wiley.

Ramos-Rodriguez, A. R., S. Martinez-Fierro, J. A. Medina-Garrido, and J. Ruiz-Navarro (2015). Global entrepreneurship monitor versus panel study of entrepreneurial dynamics: comparing their intellectual structures. *International Entrepreneurship and Management Journal 11,* 571–597.

Reiss, E. (2011). *The Lean Start-up.* New York City: Penquin Random House, Crown Business.

Reynolds, P. D. (2007). New Firm Creation in the U.S.: A PSED I Overview. *Foundations and Trends in Entrepreneurship 3*(1), 1–149.

Reynolds, P. D. (2012). Entrepreneurship in Developing Economies: The Bottom Billions and Business Creation. *Foundations and Trends in Entrepreneurship 8*(3), 141–277.

Reynolds, P. D. (2015a). Business Creation Stability: Why is it so Hard to Increase Entrepreneurship? *Foundations and Trends in Entrepreneurship 10*(5-6), 321–475.

Reynolds, P. D. (2015b). When is a Firm Born? Alternative Criteria and Consequences. *Peer Review Paper Session, Vancouver, BC, Canada, Academy of Management Annual Meeting,* 11 August.

Reynolds, P. D., N. M. Carter, W. B. Gartner, and P. G. Greene (2004). The Prevalence of Nascent Entrepreneurs in the United States: Evidence from the Panel Study of Entrepreneurial Dynamics. *Small Business Economics 43*(4), 263–284.

Reynolds, P. D. and R. T. Curtin (2009). Business Creation in the United States: Entry, Startup Activities, and the Launch of New Ventures. In *U.S. Small Business Administration, The Small Business Economy: A Report to the President 2008,* Chapter 7.

Reynolds, P. D., D. Hechavarria, L.(R). Tian, M. Samuelsson, and P. Davidsson (2016). Panel Study of Entrepreneurial Dynamics: A Five Cohort Outcomes Harmonized Data Set. *Research Gate,* DOI: 1.13140/RG.2.1.2561.7682.

Samadeni, M., M. C. Withers, and S. T. Certo (2014). The Perils of Endogeneity and Instrumental Variables in Strategy Research. *Strategic Management Journal 35*, 1070–1079.

Schoonhoven, C. B., M. D. Burton, and P. D. Reynolds (2009). Reconceiving the Gestation Window: The Consequences of Competing Definitions of Firm Conception and Birth. In P. Reynolds and R. Curtin (Eds.), *New Firm Creation in the United States: Initial Explorations with the PSED II. Data Set*, Chapter 11, pp. 219–238. NYC: Springer.

Tornikoski, E. and M. Renko (2014). Timely creation of new organizations - The imprinting effects of entrepreneurs initial founding decision. *M@n@gement 17*(3), 193–213.

Van Praag, C. M. and P. H. Versloot (2007). What is the value of entrepreneurship? A review of recent research. *Small Business Economics 29*, 351–382.

Weber, M. (1978). *Economy and Society*. Berkeley, CA: U. of California Press (Translated by Guenther Roth and Claus Wittich).

Yang, T. and H. E. Aldrich (2012). Out of sight but not of mind: Why failure to account for left truncation biases research on failure rates. *Journal of Business Venturing 27*, 477–492.

Lightning Source UK Ltd.
Milton Keynes UK
UKHW022107080223
416681UK00011B/2805